*On the Wing*

BOOKS BY NORA SAYRE

*Sixties Going On Seventies*

*Running Time: Films of the Cold War*

*Previous Convictions: A Journey Through the 1950s*

# On the Wing

A YOUNG AMERICAN ABROAD

# Nora Sayre

COUNTERPOINT
WASHINGTON, D.C.

LIBRARY OF CONGRESS CATALOGING-IN-PUBLICATION DATA
Sayre, Nora.
    On the wing : a young American abroad / Nora Sayre.
        p. cm.
    ISBN 1-58243-144-2 (alk. paper)
    1. Sayre, Nora—Childhood and youth.  2. Film critics—
United States—Biography.  3. Americans—Europe—
Biography.    I. Title.
PN1998.3.S32 A3 2001
791.43'092—DC21                                        00-065861

Jacket and text design by Amy Evans McClure

COUNTERPOINT
P.O. Box 65793
Washington, D.C. 20035–5793

Counterpoint is a member of the Perseus Books Group

10 9 8 7 6 5 4 3 2 1

*For*

*Susanna Doyle   Lis Harris   Nita Colgate*

*and*

*all the Stackpoles, with my very special thanks*

But I am sailing to Athens! *Make voyages!—Attempt them!*
Tennessee Williams, *Camino Real*

I have walked through many lives,
some of them my own . . .
Stanley Kunitz, "The Layers"

# *Prelude*

Landing in wet, green London rather by accident, I soon encountered the individuals who would themselves become my adventures. A shouting semi-paranoid Hungarian, fat men with dazzling vocabularies, a brilliant actress who rebelled against performing, a community of blacklisted American writers, a swashbuckling star on the lam from Hollywood: all of them awaited me when I left my home in New York as I turned twenty-two. They weren't mentors or models, but they were very exciting stimulants during my apprentice years, which transported me to England for the second half of the Fifties. Some of them seemed to be showing me how *not* to live, warning me away from quicksand and thunderbolts, from flattery and violence. I rarely followed their advice. But I was immensely enriched by their experiences: by the tales they told, the best and worst times they had seen.

These men and women also became my extended family, and I wanted to understand them in every way I could, above all because their lives—in the midst of wars, even revolutions—were utterly unlike anything I'd known. Yet as I absorbed their stories, what they had gone through seemed to color my own existence, and it almost seemed as if their memories became mine. Maybe it was influence by osmosis. I'd ignored both history and politics while I was growing up. But as a listener in London I gradually learned a good deal about the tidal waves of the twentieth century and how they affected private life, especially throughout World War II—which had seemed remote during my Manhattan childhood—and the Cold War.

Like millions of young Americans with knapsacks and bicycles, I carried my eagerness along with my passport. In search of a city where I would test myself and try my wings, I was swathed in self-doubt and determination: I lived with a timid recklessness, or perhaps a reckless timidity. Traveling to discover myself, I was rash and queasy. I believed in free will and in one's freedom to make choices. Yet I was titillated by the idea of destiny or destination: the nameless persons and unforeseeable events that were around the corner or over the next hill. Like most of my Harvard friends, I had a large ego and little confidence. One of them said enviously that I was "adventure-prone," which turned out to be true. And I felt a kinship with Saul Bellow's Augie March, when he said he was "adoptional"; in Europe, strangers took me up or in. Although I grew up during a pre-feminist era, it never occurred to me that a woman couldn't do what she wished or that women might not be considered the equals of men—and I was so unseasoned that it took me a while to perceive that many men thought otherwise.

Neither an Anglophile nor -phobe, I loved France and had spent a few months in Paris, but departed for London because I hadn't found a job. Later I heard that *The Herald Tribune* had phoned my lodgings just one day after I left Paris for good, ready to hire me if I could be available at once. My whole life would have been different if I'd received that call. But probably not better. In the meantime I was involved with a young American who was doing postgraduate work at Oxford; he and I commuted uneasily between that town and London. Mismatched, far from

New England where we'd first been together, we fell out of step even more quickly than we would have at home. We kept running into other young American couples whose travels were telling them how ill suited they were: quarrels in the Roman Forum, fights on the Champs-Élysées, eruptions near the bronze lions in Trafalgar Square.

Enthralled by the mystique of Europe, I was also in flight from my family in New York: from the mental illness of my mother, who was manic-depressive and suicidal, from a father I loved but whose frustrations and explosions were hard to live with at that time, from their terrible marriage, their angers and griefs. So it was imperative to earn enough to stay abroad and begin writing. Because my father was a writer—for *The New Yorker* and other magazines, as were many of his friends—I wished to start choosing my own words at a healthy distance. In a city that contained no personal memories, I was gambling on myself: to find ways of making money and living on my own terms, free of the parental past.

Henry James saw the young American woman as "the heiress of all the ages," particularly when she was in Europe. His heroines hovered at my elbow: I wasn't as naive as Daisy Miller or as willfully obtuse as Isabel Archer (James called her "an intelligent but presumptuous girl"), and never noble like Milly Theale. Yet I identified with them, with their appetite for independence. I didn't think of myself as an innocent abroad—I thought I was a worldly New Yorker—but I did know that I had a lot to learn. And I wanted to develop the "direct talent for life" that James had described.

Early on, Isabel Archer says "I'm very fond of my liberty" and "I wish to choose my own fate." Asked if she knows where she's going, she evokes a voyage into terra incognita: "A swift carriage, of a dark night, rattling with four horses over roads that one can't see—that's my idea of happiness." The sense of possibilities is thrilling: her cousin Ralph wishes "to see what she does with herself"—in his preface to *The Portrait of a Lady*, James wrote, "Well, what will she *do*?"—just as I wanted to see what I would do. Along with Isabel Archer's craving for freedom and her desire "to see, to try, to know," I shared a taste for the unknown with the narrator of Dylan Thomas's *Adventures in the Skin Trade*: "One pleasure is, Samuel said to himself, that I do not know what I expect to happen to me." In truth I was in some ways naive—too much so to be aware of it.

An apolitical aesthete, a footloose romantic, I didn't look behind me as I left my country, where the anti-Communist crusade was flourishing and conformity was king, especially among the very young; even in New York the freer spirits were wary of bucking the norm. In England I found that dissidents were shaping the culture: new novelists and playwrights, satirists of all sorts, much of the press, were shaking up the status quo. The Establishment was still full of old Etonians who shuttled between the grouse moors and their daughters' debutante balls, but their ears rang with ridicule: they were assailable as never before. And unaffiliated radicals were adept at putting pressure on the government: politicians loathed them but had to listen to them. When Ruth Ellis, who shot the abusive lover who jilted her, was hanged in the summer of 1955, the campaign against capital punishment gathered outraged momentum. So did the assaults on censorship and the exertions to reform the laws against homosexuality.

I'd been told that English manners were impeccable, but when I asked a nice-looking young man in a duffle coat for street directions, he yelled, "Piss off, you fucking cunt!" (Perhaps he was offended by an American accent.) Upper-crust dinner parties were spiced with four-letter words which were uttered largely in private in Manhattan. And in London it seemed that there were no eccentrics: I heard no one criticized for his or her behavior. In a land where desserts had names like *trifle* and *fool*, where MGM had built a medieval fortress at Elstree for the latest Walter Scott picture, only to face furious locals protesting the demolition of this lucrative tourist trap, where a tremendous strike of Fleet Street newspapers became a drunken holiday for legions of reporters—so much so that Scottish journalists came down to drink in sympathy for lost wages—it appeared that nothing could be called odd. (How the Brits drank! Awesome even to macho American foreign correspondents.) The England I was beginning to know was witty, opportunistic, literate beyond an American's imaginings, bawdy, physically uncomfortable (indoors—where chilblains were plentiful while gas fires befouled the air), and skeptical of progress. The polluted fogs were thick, choking, and clinging. The postal system was excellent and the phone service ghastly: often you got crossed lines or what sounded like a batch of people eating toast and crunching celery, but no one much seemed to mind.

And nobody I knew cared about "loss of Empire," as the Beaverbrook papers did. American pundits who claimed that Britons were mourning their imperial powers misunderstood the nature of England in the late Fifties: what did matter (hugely) to the public was the rising standard of living, full employment, and the fact that—because of the welfare state—most people didn't have to worry about money. The acute poverty of the first postwar decade had ended by the time I came to London. Tory commentators said the waxing prosperity was fueled by free enterprise and market competition. The Socialists were proud of the social programs that sustained those who had no investments. Painfully accustomed to the financial crises of middle-income Americans like my parents—whose medical bills devoured all their earnings and savings—I was amazed that their English counterparts could lead such affordable lives. The National Health Service prevented fiscal disasters, and any qualified student who needed a university scholarship or a grant could have one. And there was a strong safety net for the poorest: the most destitute families didn't go hungry or homeless.

Long-term Socialists were disappointed that the postwar Labour Party had not greatly altered the social structure of Britain. And in the midst of a democratic economy, I was slow to grasp the complexities of the class system or its wreath of superiorities. At a big Labour Party dinner at the House of Commons, where there were few women and I knew no one but my escort, the elegant wife of a Labour peer spoke kindly to me while I was tongue-tied. She asked if I had English relatives. No. "Anglo-Saxon, surely?" I said my mother's forebears had been Irish. "Oh," she exclaimed with a bright, reassuring smile, "Oh, I *count* that as Anglo-Saxon." But it took me more than a year to see how the English upper classes treated the others—mainly by trying to exclude them from Establishment jobs—because there was a widespread notion that the class system was fading amid attacks by eloquent rebels. V. S. Pritchett wrote that George Orwell had seen World War II "as a fight against the governing class as well as against the Nazis": many men didn't want to be ruled by their former officers. The yearly Aldermaston marches, where multitudes gathered in opposition to nuclear weapons, brought Britons of divergent backgrounds together: people who had never met before trooped side by side through spring rains.

As Isabel Archer's uncle says, "The advantage of being an American here is that you don't belong to any class." Still, I was irked on hearing that Americans were immature (which I was) and piggish (I wasn't). We were crude and disgustingly ambitious; our attitude was: "It's bigger! It's better! And it costs more!" Our foreign policy was idiotic and we had no history, no art. Some of the English defined us as rich uneducated clods who plundered Europe of Impressionist paintings while spreading seersucker and Coke all over the globe, promoting vulgarity and ugliness in every nation. English actors and intellectuals aped our accents by whining through their noses. But they couldn't bear American Anglophiles, such as the youngish men in three-piece Savile Row suits who ate from forks in their left hands and quoted nineteenth-century anthologies of *Punch*; the English tended to snub them brutally.

Yet other Londoners were swift to apologize for "Yank bashing" and there was abundant interest in modern American literature from Hemingway to Arthur Miller and Tennessee Williams. (They didn't appear to understand Faulkner: the decaying South, which he hated as well as loved, the ruined aristocrats and the triumph of the redneck Snopes family, the recurrent Christ figures—all seemed grotesque to English critics, who didn't fathom his monumental despair.) As a fledgling I was very protective of my American ear; I didn't want to write like the English, though I reveled in the varieties of their language and their pleasure in it.

I still pined for Paris and began to miss New York. But my London was a city of productive, questing foreigners: Central Europeans, Scandinavians, French socialists, Americans (especially Californians). I never knew the traditional English well; most of my friends, from Kensington to Hampstead, had been partly raised in other countries, and they were aliens in the world of public-school regattas, herbaceous borders, the Church of England, and canvassing for Tory candidates. In my London there were feasts of Mediterranean food, gleaming red pimentos and black olives, evenings of American folk songs, festivals of Italian movies, cheers for Bertolt Brecht's visiting theater troupe from East Berlin, and celebrations of the Swedish holiday Saint Lucia's Day, when young girls wore crowns of lighted candles. On Thanksgiving, several *New Statesman* writers insisted on buying me a turkey sandwich in a Chelsea pub. I was learning that the English liked strangers: to be brand-new in London was delightful. The residents knew one another too well and they welcomed an unfamiliar face.

London was still a very white city, lacking the ethnic influences and multicultural riches—Asian, Muslim, Caribbean, African—affecting English fiction, theater, music, and painting today. The British "colour bar," England's term for racism, was denounced but not widely discussed; it was believed that "the problem" belonged largely to "prejudiced" Americans. Surely the public was unaware that shortly before Winston Churchill left office in 1955, when "coloured immigration" was expanding, he advised the Cabinet that "Keep England White" would be a useful campaign slogan for the Tories.

As I recall those London years, I'm examining the connections between private lives and public events. I'm also concerned with education—that of a young American in a country dramatically unlike her own—and the mingling of international cultures before the eyes of a shy adventurer. But my American frame of reference did not change when I was settled abroad. And as I grew homesick, I became more American.

Yet I also became intrigued by the mid-century history of Britain and Europe, which hadn't mattered to me before. This was the era of Khrushchev's horrific revelations of Stalin's crimes, of the Suez invasion and the Hungarian revolution. It was a time of historic turning points: at an Arkansas high school, nine black pupils were threatened with death by a white mob; Sputnik circled the earth; Castro seized power in Cuba. At home the young were isolated by the atmosphere of the Cold War, which had caused most schools and universities to keep silent about politics, apart from firing teachers said to be un-American. But students were not meant to be much aware of that.

In those days, youth wasn't admired in the fashion it is now, and being young seemed to mean being ignorant, being raw. Hence I was avid to enter the domain of people at least ten years ahead of me or twice my age: that was where passion and magic thrived, or so I believed; that's where the prizes were. This portion of personal history takes me to the age of twenty-six, when—to my surprise—my life still seemed as fluid as it had been a few years before. In the Fifties, Americans were presumed to be fully adult by their mid-twenties. (A youthful way of living that lasted up to or past thirty was frowned on until the Sixties.) "Maturity" eluded me, and perhaps dwelling overseas kept me and many of my compatriots younger than we were supposed to be: amid the cafés of the Saint-Germain or the leafy streets of Chelsea, some of us enjoyed a prolonged adolescence.

Recently there has been much confusion about the distinctions between autobiography and memoir. The former is usually the chronicle of a whole life, commencing with childhood, and it concentrates on the author's character and development. A memoir—like this book—isn't necessarily *about* the writer but is devoted to events he or she has witnessed and individuals the writer has known. Of course the two forms are sometimes combined. After all, most published works apart from the phone book contain passages of autobiographical writing; critics and biographers often expose more of themselves than they intended. So may historians: Alfred Kazin observed that Gibbon's *Decline and Fall of the Roman Empire* "is all about how important he was." Still, some of the newish "memoirs" seem to deserve the honorable name of fiction rather than claiming to be true.

Currently a memoir is expected to feature a disaster, to be shocking or suffused with misery—especially if it's written by a woman. Buckets of boohoo follow the disemboweling divorces, the abortions, the limbs lost in accidents, the cruel mothers, sexually demanding fathers, attempted suicides, rapes, muggings, booze, drugs, cancer, infertility, illegitimacy, projectile vomiting, incest, marital mayhem, too much or too little sex, lousy sex, manic depression, skin eruptions, and learning disabilities. Let me stress that I'm not making light of tragedy or suffering. No life I know has been untouched by them. In fiction and the theater, from Ophelia and the Duchess of Malfi to Ahab and Lily Bart and Willy Loman, there are sufferers who enlighten us— about ourselves and our society—and so do some talented contemporary memoirists. But I'm impatient with the idea that a narrative has value only if the narrator is wretched.

In the age of the Internet there are no more secrets—not even that mole on your inner thigh or your affair with your spouse's best friend. When the tone is penitent, this has been called "couch writing," as though it's addressed to the unseen analyst. Admittedly, certain memoirs are confessions more than lamentations; the writers are flogging themselves for their deeds: seducing a child, kleptomania for which another person was punished, self-mutilation. Yet why do some masochistic accounts sound boastful? Maybe because a writer who asks to be disliked feels significant? Entitled to rouse a reader's strongest emotions. Or perhaps because the writer has a captive audience, as long as a pair of eyes stays on the page. The writer who seems to be shouting "Hate me: I deserve it" may bask in the vision of a reader's rapt attention—when a friend or relative might flee.

Yet as one of Henry James's characters exclaims, "The subject doesn't matter, it's the treatment, the treatment!" The topic may not be crucial. But calamity can invite clichés: exhausted or lazy language is frequently used to express pain. Banality beckons from the depths of sorrow: "Love left me bleeding," "My heart contracted," "There my innocence died." Happiness can even cause a heart to "overflow." Surely hearts are best omitted from autobiographies or memoirs: they tend to sound soggy.

I'm not squeamish: elsewhere I've written about how my mother slashed her wrists, throat, and ankles in our bathtub—afterward there was blood on our bathroom ceiling and I was told that people who slit their wrists often fling their arms upward—about my undergraduate abortion, frighteningly illegal in those days (the doctor feared that policemen might burst in to arrest or blackmail her), about the breakdowns of some of my family's closest friends. But in this book I choose to revive a young explorer's beginnings, the first voyage taken into the world. I want readers to retrieve their own beginnings—leaving home or

exchanging a small town for an electrifying city, a familiar landscape for an exotic foreign vista. I want them to think of the first
steps, the mistakes and the astonishments. I want them to think
of starting out—in a place that held many surprises or among
people who captured their imaginations. So this is a book of
chances and changes—of the sort that startle us when life is new.

Graham Greene said that one of his motives for writing his
autobiography was "a hungry curiosity": he assumed that revisiting the past would help to explain it, would give order to "the
chaos of experience." Because much of memory is visual, you may
find that recalling the fern wallpaper in the since-demolished
bedroom of an early love or sunlight sparkling on a certain river
can clarify the events of the time, illuminate your buried feelings.
A skyscraper's shadow can remind you of the walks you took
within it—with someone you haven't seen in years but can at last
understand. The sound of late apples and pears falling on muddy
autumn earth may make you think of the person you fled from
after one turbulent season.

Greene rebuked his friends for the habit of "self-defense"
when they wrote about their lives: employing irony to deride the
passions of young adulthood, hence forestalling "cruel criticism."
I understand that temptation. Like many only children, I've often
stood somewhat apart, watching and eavesdropping, amused by
irony, whether it was my own or rooted in a situation. At times I
used irony as armor. Yet on the page I've tried to be faithful to
my youthful emotions; even if they vanished later, they were
powerful while they existed. And although I'm allergic to sentimentality, I found that I wished to write about romantic love:
certainly it's nourished by imagination, but it is not imaginary;
it's genuine though rarely permanent. (Woody Allen said unre-
quited love is the only kind that lasts.)

People without siblings are also attuned to privacy, which I
equated with freedom—at least until someone said that privacy
should be shared. Here a paradoxical stimulant is at work (or

play). Some of us who love privacy choose to share what we have seen with strangers, convinced that it will excite them—and make us fascinating to them. An ample ego is indispensable in writing this kind of history, even if it doesn't focus on one's own viscera.

The dead won't stay that way: springing up in our memories, they can jolt us with their vitality. In this book I want to honor some of them—in the context of what mattered most to them. And as I've remembered the men and women who captivated (or alarmed) me in my early twenties, I'm writing about what moved, charmed, or appalled me in human nature—in any country. Through letters and notebooks I've relived what made me laugh or shiver, dash forward or recoil. As the director and theater critic Harold Clurman said of his memoir *All People Are Famous*, it is "about myself through others." By training the spotlight on other individuals, or by taking a tour of their interiors, you may also reveal a great deal about yourself.

# I.

I was appalled to hear his voice. As Arthur Koestler hissed instructions at me through a small intercom in his door frame, I wished I might evaporate—or that he would. Standing in the darkness on his doorstep in Knightsbridge, I yearned to be in another city, almost regretting the journey that had brought me to this place.

Hunting for work, starting to write, I knew almost no one in England except the young man at Oxford. But I was sustained by anticipation: I expected enormous rewards and ongoing nourishment from an immersion in ancient civilizations and the arts: literature, theater, and the paintings and sculptures of Europe were going to shape my character and mind as well as my sensibilities. "Now shall I make my soul, compelling it to study": Yeats wrote those lines when he was sixty-one, but they spoke to me at twenty-two; my voyage abroad was meant to be an act of self-creation as much as an exploration of the world. Meanwhile I lived in one small room with a creaky floor in a South Kensington bed-sitter, where I slept on khaki sheets (postwar army surplus), awoke to see a washstand disguised to look exactly like a washstand (zigzag carpentry), a gas ring, a black metal box where a shilling purchased heat and light (when the coin expired with a click, the electric fire and the lights went out), and what a friend called Caliban's breakfast: a fried egg swimming so deep in grease that it swirled around the plate, and a dead tomato.

Edmund Wilson, my family's friend since my childhood, had written to his friend Celia Paget Goodman, a magazine editor who had worked for the wartime Information Research Department of the Foreign Office, that I was newly arrived in London. I didn't know that he'd been in love with her twin sister, who had married Arthur Koestler and parted from him before her death. In my early twenties I was moving beneath a web of my seniors' tangled relationships, sometimes unaware of the threads or the ruptures. Celia, a small, direct, and charming woman with amused eyes, took a rapid look at my fraying college wardrobe and deduced that I needed employment right away. She said I should consult her brother-in-law. I said I couldn't; to me Koestler seemed to be a colossus. (Like millions of American students of that era, I'd read *Darkness at Noon*, his exposé of the Soviet purges, in high school, where it was almost a textbook: the novel was essential to the Cold War education of several generations.) Celia Goodman grinned and said that while he was perfectly horrible in many ways, he was sympathetic to young people who needed to earn: he remembered very well what that was like. Next day she rang and told me that since she knew I wouldn't contact him, she'd arranged for me to have a drink with him; she quite gleefully said I would not be able to cancel because she wouldn't give me the phone number.

Shivery with spring flu, groggy from big red pills called Quinasps (quinine and aspirin), I was relieved to see that his house on Montpelier Square was completely dark when I got there. He must have forgotten, so I needn't meet him at all. Still, I ought to ring the bell—just so I could tell Celia that I had. A long silence. As I started to leave, a voice shouted—almost screamed—"*Who is that?*" through the door phone. The accent was riddled with *v*'s and *s*'s and *z*'s. I gasped my name, then the voice ordered me to push various buttons and levers on the right and left of the door—which would eventually open. Then, the voice said, I would find myself in a totally dark hallway. I was to stretch out my hands and grope forward until I touched a bannister; I should grasp it and "feel, feel, feel" my way upstairs, then reach for the wall on my left and feel, feel, feel my way along it, find a doorknob, enter a dark room, turn on the light and wait. I felt as though the Minotaur might be lurking at the center of the labyrinth.

Sweating from more than flu, I stumbled blindly through black space, clutched the bannister, then hugged the wall, and lurched into the room. What the light revealed was almost shocking: cozy chintz upholstery, comfortable chairs, a Courbet cow over the fireplace. The house remained utterly silent, you would have thought it was empty. Terror subsiding, cheered by the cow, I sank into a sofa.

More silence. After half an hour I grew restless and began to sift through a pile of *Encounter*s. Finally there was a rustling sound and a musky, spicy scent (Bellodgia, I later learned), footsteps in the hall; the door opened and an astounding couple walked in. He was short with a large head and broad shoulders: when he sat down, he appeared to be taller than he was, and his dinner jacket seemed to give him height. Enveloped in black silk and lace, she was a luminous beauty with huge moth eyes, shining short dark hair, celestial cheekbones, a delicate curving smile.

Much younger than he. I realized that they were probably in bed when I rang the bell and had needed time to dress for a grand dinner party.

Koestler was genial, no longer barking or hissing. She— Elizabeth Jane Howard, whose novels I would soon admire— nodded encouragement. He handed us gin and tonics and asked what kind of work I was seeking and what I had studied in college, year by year. As I told him about our vast historical surveys and freshman humanities courses, he beamed and seized on the subjects. It seemed that he enjoyed sweeping cultural definitions, also syntheses: "Seventeenth-century man was the man of science and philosophy. Eighteenth-century man was the man of *reason*. Nineteenth-century man was the man of *feeling* [veeling]. Twentieth-century man is the *zynsezis* of all these." He pronounced "zynsezis" with such gusto that it seemed logical that he subsequently married a woman named Zynsia (Cynthia). He extolled London as an international city and said I would prosper there, adding, "London is the salvation of Americans," before we walked down the brightly lit staircase and they hurtled off into the night in his small MG.

I felt as if I'd passed through a masonic rite: trial by mystery and darkness and fear, then redemption through light and a quickening potion. Soon thereafter I was told that his complex security system was a consequence of being jailed in Franco's Spain, where he had heard the cries of other prisoners—mostly young peasants—as they were led to their executions while he was in solitary confinement. As a known Communist, he expected to be shot, though it was never clear if Franco had signed the death warrant. After ninety-five days Koestler was released from his cell in Seville. Prominent British politicians had obtained his freedom in exchange for another prisoner. But for years after *Darkness at Noon* he was certain that he was on the Russians' hit list.

I began to find work, mainly research on American history. In my dusty Queen's Gate bed-sitter, where I competed for the pay phone on the stair landing with Mr. Hanrahan, an unemployed Irish journalist who struck matches on his thigh, I read at length about the battle of Shiloh, the second-worst battle in our Civil War. I wrote a detailed account for a biographer of Henry Morton Stanley (author of *How I Found Livingston*), who was said to have been a habitual liar. He had covered the battle for *The New York Herald*, but the biographer wasn't sure if Stanley had been there, and it appeared that he had made errors.

In the midst of Shiloh I was invited to tea by the literary scholar and editor John Hayward, T. S. Eliot's friend and flat-mate on Cheyne Walk. Crippled by muscular dystrophy, impos-ing in his wheelchair, Hayward had deformed hands and his clearly enunciated sentences issued from a misshapen mouth: his huge swollen underlip seemed to float out independently from his lower jaw. I'd been told that he looked like a duckbill platypus and that he liked to talk about sex because it was impos-sible for him. He spoke of statements in the yellow press from young women who had been raped in Hyde Park—"'He threw me on the grass verge and interfered with me'—why is it always the *verge,* I wonder?," prostitutes in Shepherd's Market, John George Haigh (the acid-bath murderer with a toothbrush mus-tache who'd pretended to market false fingernails and had lived in the Onslow Court Hotel, near my bed-sitter), and the possible virginity of a young American woman who was keeping com-pany with William Faulkner: "Do you think that old corncob Faulkner has given Miss X her sanctuary?"

John Hayward had no work for me, but the next day Mr. Hanrahan pounded excitedly on my door: Arthur Koestler was on the hallway phone. In clipped tones he said, "I have not found you a job. I have found you a flat." (He disapproved of bedsitters.) Again there was mystery: he named no landlord but gave me incredibly convoluted tube and bus directions to 6 Blomfield Road in Little Venice. He told me to open the wooden gate but *not* to ring at the dark red upper door, walk down the path but do *not* enter the garden, find the door beneath the stairs, "and someone will answer." That someone turned out to be the gracious Elizabeth Jane Howard, known as Jane, eager to rent a large bedroom with a view of the Regency Canal for two and a half pounds a week. On long summer evenings, sunlight bounced off the water and shone through the leaves of a willow tree. Books, ranged neatly on shelves, seemed to be the skeleton of the house. In Jane's living room a scarlet carpet glowed between pale yellow walls; when the French doors were open, a large gilt-framed oval mirror reflected the greenest of gardens. I almost expected that mirror to slide back and reveal a series of secret rooms. The dining room had crimson flocked wallpaper and a small golden creature (maybe a griffin) at the top of the window frame. It was—and in memory still is—one of the most beautiful houses I've seen.

Part of the time Jane lived with Koestler, but I was soon drawn into her household, which sometimes included her witty younger brother Colin, who'd just gotten his degree at Cambridge. He and I pulled a few weeds from the garden, ate potted shrimps and cold rare beef, and played Jane's Scarlatti and Mozart records while she was in Montpelier Square. He had extremely strong wrists, and Jane said we should screw him to the kitchen wall so that he would always be there to open jars of olives or nuts. She used to leave the house full of roses and the fridge crammed with pâté, roast chicken, and cream. When she was at home, a stream of terrifically attractive men came for lunch and dinner. One of my favorites was a tall, doleful barrister whom Colin and I called Mr. Lost Cause; hopelessly in love with Jane despite what she referred to as "a perfectly good mistress," he was permitted to pick small stones out of the lawn while she planted phlox and delphiniums and told him about her troubles with Koestler, who had a long history of brutality toward women.

Because Jane was ten years my senior, dashing and magnetic, the author of novels praised for their delectable ironies, their portraits of tortuous marriages and scenes of fleeting enchantment, I was slow to see that she was short on self-esteem. The women in her books were often punished for their romanticism; in pursuit of love, they were sexually adventurous but usually disappointed by the men who enjoyed their bodies while deriding their feelings. Most were elegant masochists. Jane's first two novels, *The Beautiful Visit* and *The Long View*, were compared to Rosamond Lehmann's, but to me her writing seemed to belong in the tradition of Elizabeth Bowen and Elizabeth Taylor, attuned to Evelyn Waugh. The pessimism in her work coexisted with a splendid sense of the ridiculous. I felt that Jane Austen would have appreciated her books: both of them portrayed really rotten behavior in the midst of bittersweet comedy.

Jane Howard was a temperate Tory, and she seemed to have a strong sense of justice—not social or political but rooted in her concept of decency and honesty. One of her admirers referred to her "speaking glances and glancing speeches," but I found her forthright. Still, I learned that she was as anxious as she was glamorous; she looked sure of herself yet wasn't. At nineteen she had married the naturalist and ornithologist Peter Scott, the sour son of Scott of the Antarctic; his paintings of birds (especially wildfowl in flight) were widely reproduced on place mats. They had one daughter. Long divorced, Jane seemed to be quarry for mordant men whose energies and language captivated her; in her future there were such mercurial lovers as Kenneth Tynan and Romain Gary; her third ex-husband would be Kingsley Amis. She was a loyal person who appeared to inspire disloyalty. Yet in the midst of pain—lavishly dispensed by Koestler—she seemed to savor life's pleasures more than many people: music, her garden, memories of the Côte d'Azur, Sussex, her brother's jokes, salmon trout, and cold orange soufflé seemed to enhance an existence suffused with suffering. Years later I thought of her when the poet Philip Larkin said that unhappiness was a stimulus for his writing: "Deprivation is for me what daffodils were for Wordsworth."

Life under Jane's roof was novelistic: that is, it was like being *in* a novel rather than just reading one. But there were lulls between chapters when she was away. In her absence I spread papers and old news clippings all over her scarlet rug, working on my knees because the desk was too small. I was doing research on the Loch Ness monster for James Thurber, who was spending part of the summer in London. He and I were as intrigued by the hoaxes as by the most reputable sightings, and he developed a theory that the monster was hardly ever seen because it was so shocked by its first glimpse of a human being that it preferred to stay under water. In the fourth century, Celts were converted to Christianity when the creature surfaced. (In 1940 an Italian fascist paper, *Popolo d'Italia*, claimed that it had been killed by a direct hit during the blitz.) Because I had to reregister as an alien every six months and needed a legal reason to remain in England, Thurber gave me a letter saying that I was engaged in research for him on the Scottish kings before Macbeth—he thought that could go on for years.

Next I was hired by BBC Radio to gather factual material on American crime; the producer who interviewed me put a box of raspberries on the table between us and asked, "Do you use these?" For a documentary program on Dutch Schultz (aka Arthur Flegenheimer) and Abe (Kid Twist) Reles, I became an overnight expert on Murder, Inc., the death squad of the Syndicate, staying a few days ahead of the scriptwriters, who were enamored of their notion of gangland slang. They asked me what a canary was. Stool pigeon I said. But they confused that with a sweet potato, and I saw the script barely in time to correct lines like, "Whoa, Mac, hold your horses or I'll flip you."

Schultz, a tycoon of the New York numbers racket, was pronounced Public Enemy Number One by J. Edgar Hoover in
1934. The gangster had planned to assassinate Thomas E. Dewey,
Manhattan special prosecutor, in 1935. But members of the
Syndicate decided that Schultz himself must be bumped off,
since the killing of Dewey would spur a nationwide crackdown
on the mob. Schultz was shot in the men's room of a saloon in
Newark; this created problems for the BBC scriptwriters and
technicians. First the actor had to say, "I'm going to . . ." The can,
I suggested. No, British audiences might not understand. The
john? Same objection. Finally it was called *the gents.* So that
Schultz wouldn't seem to be pissing, he said he wanted to "wash
my hands" and there was dialogue over the sink: "Would you
pass me the *soap?*" But the running water sounded as though he
was in the center of a cyclone; even when it was toned down, he
seemed to be taking a bath. I was grateful when the shots rang
out, but the actors were sorry: they loved their frightful pseudo-
Brooklyn accents. The second part of the "documentary" focused
on Reles, a vital informer on Murder, Inc., who fell or was
thrown out of a window of a Coney Island hotel in 1941. The program was called "The Canary Who Could Sing But Couldn't
Fly." Because I had no work permit, the BBC—which was funded by the government—paid me illegally under the table: wads
of pound notes were pressed into my hands when no one was
looking.

In the meantime I was reading a lot of Sartre and Camus;
Koestler called them "the Little Flirts of the St. Germain." I gathered that they had once been friends of his, and in the midst of
my enthusiasm for their plays and novels I was startled by his disdain. He also made scathing remarks about Sartre's rapproche-
ment with the French Communists in the early Fifties (which
ended after the Russians' invasion of Hungary in 1956). I turned
to *The Invisible Writing,* the second volume of Koestler's autobiography, and also brushed up on his background. He was born in

Budapest in 1905 to Jewish parents; when he was nine the family moved to Vienna, where he was raised. As a university student of engineering, he became a keen Zionist, then spent two years in Palestine as a reporter for Berlin newspapers, moving to Germany just as the Nazis were gaining strength. Appalled that the Socialist Party had failed to halt the fascist tide, he studied Marxism and became a Communist on the last day of 1931, viewing the Party as "the only apparent alternative to Nazi rule."

Visiting the Soviet Union in 1932–33, he saw the terrible famine caused by forced collectivization in the Ukraine. But he accepted the official explanation that the millions of starving peasants were reactionaries who'd resisted collectivization and therefore had to be evicted from their farms. Since Hitler had come to power, Koestler couldn't return to Germany so he settled in Paris. He made three trips to Spain, covering the Spanish Civil War for the British *News Chronicle*; his arrest occurred on his third visit. Back in Paris, he resigned from the Party in 1938, propelled by the Soviet purges and the Comintern's vicious assaults on independent leftists in Spain. When the war began he was incarcerated for four months in France as an "undesirable alien," then released due to international pressures. As the Germans advanced, he was prompted by a Jean Gabin movie to enlist in the Foreign Legion as a way of escaping from France; on arrival in England he was immediately imprisoned for several weeks in a detention camp for aliens. Despite that confinement, he would become a fervent Anglophile.

*Darkness at Noon* was published in 1940. His depiction of the jailing, interrogation, and execution of old Bolsheviks—through a character partly modeled on Nikolai Bukharin, Leon Trotsky, and Karl Radek—was one of the first accounts of Stalin's terrorism to reach a worldwide audience. Today, when the chronicles of mass murder have been known to millions for over fifty years, we should try to envision the novel's impact at a time when many still hoped that the Soviet Union was a just—even admirable—

society. Portraying a regime that was slaughtering its own citizens, *Darkness at Noon* was a milestone in the political landscape of the evolving Cold War. Of the men who made the Russian Revolution of 1917, Koestler wrote, "They dreamed of power with the object of abolishing power; of ruling over the people only to wean them of the habit of being ruled. All their thoughts became deeds and their dreams were fulfilled. Where were they? Their brains, which had changed the course of the world, had each received a charge of lead. Some in the forehead, some in the back of the neck."

In England the novel was very favorably reviewed by George Orwell in the *New Statesman* and championed by Kingsley Martin, the magazine's editor. The English Marxist John Strachey said the book "broke friendships, split families" on the Left. Still, the British sales were negligible. But when *Darkness at Noon* was published in the United States in 1942, it became a colossal bestseller, as it did in France. And it was said that the French Communist Party kept buying all available copies in local stores and destroying them; therefore more editions were printed and Koestler was enriched by the Party's funds.

Koestler's memoirs, including his essay in *The God That Failed*, reveal that by the time he was thirty-five he'd dwelled in a world of minefields and barbed wire, spies and assassins, suicides, torture, gas chambers, and firing squads. Hitler and Stalin had killed most of his friends. Masks and deceptions of all sorts had been essential to a European Communist—a participant in the "secret revolutionary movement"—in Germany and after the fall of France, and he'd had to hide his sympathy for the Trotskyists in Spain.

His experiences seemed "abnormal" to some British reviewers of the mid-Forties, but he retorted that "the life I have described was indeed, up to 1940, the typical case-history of a Central-European member of the intelligentsia in the totalitarian age. It was entirely normal for a writer, an artist, a politician, or a

teacher with a minimum of integrity to have several narrow escapes from Hitler and/or Stalin, to be chased and exiled. . . . It
was by no means abnormal for them, in the early thirties, to regard Fascism as the main threat, and to be attracted in varying
degrees to the great social experiment in Russia." Even after he
had come to hate the consequences of that experiment, he wrote
that being converted to Communism in the Thirties "was a sincere and spontaneous expression of an optimism born of despair;
an abortive revolution of the spirit, a misfired Renaissance. . . .
To be attracted to the new faith was, I still believe, an honorable
error. We were wrong for the right reasons."

Like many of my middle-class contemporaries I'd grown up
without a substantial sense of evil. For sheltered young postwar Americans, the concept of evil was rather abstract: it didn't
seem like a part of human nature or rooted in the natural world,
and Iago's "motiveless malignity" appeared remote. Only Hitler
and "the Japanese" were truly wicked; even so, they were aberra-
tions, somehow separate from the rest of humanity—for those of
us who were still children when the war ended, when Russia
was still an ally. We knew very well that the Nazis had tortured
Jews, had murdered them—and many who tried to help them.
Nonetheless years would pass before the enormity of the Holo-
caust became fully clear to people whose parents—like mine—
had hidden magazines featuring photographs of concentration
camps from their children; much of my generation was protected
from recent history. (Any adolescent understands suffering,
though little about tragedy.) But reading Koestler afresh, along
with Graham Greene's *Brighton Rock,* brought evil most vividly
alive, convincing me not only of its existence but that it had no
nationality.

Koestler's indictments of Stalin and the postwar Eastern
European governments were irrefutable. But as Orwell noted,
Koestler failed to find "any political position" other than anti-
Communism after his break with the Party. In time he went

overboard in denouncing independent radicals and liberals; his relations with the non-Communist Left deteriorated as he declared that those who weren't aggressive anti-Communists endangered freedom everywhere. As a fervid Cold Warrior he kept envisioning links between Bolshevism and liberalism, stating that the sentimentality and "utopianism" of liberals had enabled Communism to expand in the West. Certain that individuals, like nations, must "choose" between Communism and anti-Communism, he proclaimed that "neutrality" would be like "neutrality toward the bubonic plague." Many remarked that his obsessive anti-Communism became even more irrational as he grew older.

When I met Koestler, an American of my generation could hardly imagine what a desirable society the Soviet Union had once seemed to promise. Long afterward I wondered if his post-Communist political passions had been partially fueled by guilt: for having been as devout as he was blinkered, for having believed that "the end really justifies the means." In the mid-Thirties he'd told himself that he was working for "the happiness of all mankind." By 1941 his books were filled with betrayals, along with his own bitterness at having been betrayed. But I suspected that he also cherished his guilt: it gave him momentum.

As I would learn, his greatest gifts were for journalism, essays, and memoirs rather than fiction. Science and philosophy were the fields that mattered most to him. The searing moral and historical insights of *Darkness at Noon* gave the book its immense power, but it was a horrifying melodrama rather than a work of literature. V. S. Pritchett wrote in *Horizon* that the novel "ought to be a tragedy"; instead it was "an intellectual thriller," mainly because Koestler lacked the imaginative skills to invent characters who became more than allegorical figures. But the last two volumes of his autobiography, *Arrow in the Blue* and *The Invisible Writing*, were triumphs of story-telling by an adventurer who had most personally experienced the convulsions of the twentieth century, who knew how often the inner life was intertwined with public events. The twenty-year-old Zionist selling lemonade in the streets of Haifa, the ardent young Communist working for Willy Münzenberg (a Swiss-German director of the Comintern), the driver for Party gunmen who shot at Nazis in their Berlin taverns, the international sleuth tracking the crimes of Stalin, the man on the spot or on the run, the vagrant political exile: all came dramatically alive in books that seethed with passions and doubts, commitments and renunciations.

Some years before I knew Koestler, he had helped to create the Congress of Cultural Freedom, founded in 1950 to show that intellectuals of "the free world" were staunch anti-Communists who would defend Western culture against the Kremlin's propagandists, especially those who charged that the United States was "racist" and "fascist." Asserting that "the words 'socialism' and 'capitalism,' 'left,'and 'right'" had become meaningless, Koestler had sometimes behaved as if the "survival" of the West depended on the strength and efficiency of the Congress. There were those who felt that he was actually attacking intellectual freedom—because he showed no respect for the expression of ideas he did not share. And as the historian Christopher Lasch later wrote, "cultural freedom has consistently been confused with American propaganda"—hence it wasn't astonishing to learn one day that the Congress had been secretly funded by the CIA for sixteen years. (Koestler knew about the funding and said he "had no objection" to it.)

Koestler had lived in the "delectable nightmare" of the United States for a couple of years; there he warned Republicans that Joseph McCarthy was giving American anti-Communism a bad name in Europe, and declared himself "simply allergic to American liberals." Contemptuous of the acute commercialism and naïveté of the American literary world, he was puzzled by the state of a nation that seemed to be either in the midst of puberty or close to decay, afflicted with growing pains or senility.

He hadn't liked Clement Attlee's Labour government, but Winston Churchill had returned to power before Koestler resettled in England. And he did appreciate the liberation of Britain's colonies under both parties: in 1954 he wrote, "For the first time in history we see an empire dissolving with dignity and grace. The rise of this empire was not an edifying story: its decline is."

By the time I rang his doorbell in 1955, he had announced that his days of political activity were over and he'd started to research the book that would become *The Sleepwalkers: A History of Man's Changing Vision of the Universe*. Colin and I were told that he required quantities of privacy and silence. As Jane began to spend more nights and days in Blomfield Road, I hastily removed my Loch Ness and Murder, Inc., papers from her living-room floor. Evidently Koestler was easing her out of Montpelier Square, known as Bachelor's Fortress or BF among his male friends. (That summer he wrote in his notebook, "I can neither live alone or with somebody.") Already wounded by the accumulating rejections, Jane found that she was pregnant. Whether he knew it or merely guessed it, he grew more and more elusive when she tried to see him alone.

Finally she arranged to have supper with him after a literary barrister's big June party at Eaton Square, to which he didn't offer to take her. I'd been invited on my own, and I was having a fine time talking with Isaiah Berlin about Edmund Wilson: Berlin said, "He is the hero of my middle age!" I was entranced by Berlin's way of speaking; Alan Bennett has compared it to a Yorkshire spring called the Ebbing and Flowing Well, "which bubbles upward and falls back," much as Berlin's words did, "overflowing from his mouth, rather like a baby bringing back its food." But Koestler closed in, whispering that I must leave to dine with him and Henry Yorke (the novelist Henry Green),

whom I hadn't met. Politely I refused, knowing that Jane ought
to be with him by herself. He beckoned me aside, muttering that
I could see "that little Baltic Jew" another time, that he would be
furious if I didn't come *at once.* He was somewhat drunk. Realizing that Jane would have no chance for a tête-à-tête, I yielded to
his wrathful scowls.

Henry Green had a long mournful face and a mild gleam in
his deep-set eyes; I caught a whiff of the deadpan wit that permeated his novel *Loving.* Clearly he had no idea that Jane would
soon arrive at Montpelier Square, where Koestler gave us drinks
before squatting and plunging his head and shoulders into his gigantic hi-fi set, attempting to adjust the sound system. Only his
buttocks and legs were visible when Jane entered the living
room—she shot me a look of anger and despair, while I mouthed,
"I couldn't help it." She wore a turquoise silk shirt: a brave blaze
of color. Amid the pings and thumps from his loudspeakers,
Koestler remained halfway inside his machine, later insisting
that he had never heard Jane say, "What in *hell* is going on?"
When he emerged, he pantomimed surprise on seeing her, claiming that he'd forgotten she was coming.

Desperately she drew him onto the landing, when Green—
who had been almost completely silent—spoke. He said Koestler
was a dear friend of his, but that he was capable of great cruelty,
especially toward women, and he himself didn't want to be a part
of it. He hardly knew Jane—"a beautiful half-drowned mer-
maid"—but he aimed to forestall her humiliation. Plainly
Koestler didn't wish to see her in private, so he'd dragged us
along; moreover he liked to make outrageous scenes in front of
an audience, he wanted witnesses. But that, Green told me, was
not going to happen. He would tell a whole series of hilarious stories—some about his recent trip to Russia—"And you, ducky,
are going to laugh." He said that although we had never met before and might never meet again, we would be partners tonight,

collaborators to foil Koestler. He added that if we left now, Koestler would surely walk out on Jane.

The four of us went to an "Elizabethan" restaurant in South Kensington. Despite the waiter's entreaties, Green refused to order mead, predicting that it would be disgusting. The food, which was slow to be served, was ponderous and sticky. Lots of gristle, it clung to my teeth. I was wearing an ivory cotton brocade dress—gesturing with his wine glass, Koestler spilled claret on my knee, leaving a small permanent stain. Green talked brilliantly, Koestler drank ceaselessly, and Jane (very pale) smiled somberly at the punch lines. Koestler told one long awful joke about golf and sex—something about getting into "the wrong hole"—and Green parodied a parson's prim revulsion: "Arthur, dear, you've *gone too far.*"

Back to Green's Knightsbridge house for nightcaps. Whenever I was alone with one of the three, he or she talked urgently about the others and gave instructions, Jane telling me on the stairs not to leave yet, Koestler hissing when she was out of the room that I must stay for a while, but he would give me a pound for a taxi when he signaled me to leave. I resisted the pound. He lowered his voice, saying that he understood me very well, that I wanted freedom—"and that is good. But you cannot have freedom wizout *zisss!*" Rubbing his fingertips together, hand held high, he then clenched a pound note in his fist and kept thumping it on my thigh—"Take it! Take it!" I took it.

At last Jane and Koestler departed. Green was exuberant: he had prevented the horrendous scene that Koestler had wanted us to watch. By now Koestler was extremely drunk: he wouldn't have the gumption to torment her further tonight. I told Green about the pound and put it on his coffee table: it was crumpled into the shape of a frog. Out of nowhere Green said it was a pity that Koestler had never had children: a child might have liked that frog. (I didn't know that Koestler had refused to have chil-

dren with each of his wives—he was sure they would interfere
with his work—or that a married woman had had a child of his;
he declined to see his newborn daughter more than once, though
he did keep a few snapshots in the bottom drawer of his desk.)
Green spoke fleetingly of his own son, Sebastian—"Arrows, you
know"—pointing his index fingers toward his breast.

That evening Green had talked a lot in what a friend called
his "silken, silver-spoon voice"; hearing its graceful cadences, I
sensed that he was also a superb listener: that was clear from the
dialogue in his books. Now the voice became a bit weary; he said
he would have one more drink and then put me in a cab, because
after that "I will become very drunk, as I do every night." He explained that some people thought he drank because he wrote less
and less, while others said the drinking helped to block his writing. (His final novel had been published three years before. In the
Fifties he still liked to spend hours in pubs, eavesdropping on
conversations, but later his friends called him a hermit. Angus
Wilson would write in Green's obituary that, like Virginia Woolf,
"he walked on the thinnest of ice, on the cliff-edge of despair.")
He finished the drink with a gentle, mocking flourish, predicting that the next one would hit him very hard, paid my taxi
driver in advance, advising me to keep Koestler's pound note—
"for an exhibit"—and I rode off thinking him the kindest man
in London.

Next day I woke to the blues; I was accustomed to emotional
violence as I'd known it in my ill mother, but this was the first
time I'd seen one person determined to make another suffer. I
was beginning to believe—as I still do—that while masochists
are plentiful, sadists are quite scarce, hence they can find a slew
of victims in a lifetime. I didn't yet know that Koestler was a
manic-depressive, that the outbursts and the wild swings between rage and elation signified more than an abandonment of
control. (Earlier he'd admitted in his diary that he was sometimes
"enslaved" by "alcoholic schizophrenia.")

In *Darkness at Noon* he had written that Rubashov had perceived that "perhaps reason alone was a defective compass which led one on such a winding, twisted course that the goal finally disappeared in the mist." Surely Koestler was also writing about himself. Yet reason was rarely his guide. The savage quarrels that wrecked some of his friendships—clearly he relished fights and could almost incite others to near-riot—had cost him quite a few political allies. For him combat seemed like exercise, and he couldn't understand why others loathed it. There were ex-friends who thought him partially mad. Yet much of his behavior seemed deliberate, and he often toyed with others' reflexes. Subsequently I was told that he'd been a patient of two psychiatrists—a Freudian and a Jungian—at the same time without telling them, waiting to see which one was most disturbed when Koestler talked from the other's point of view. And it seemed to me that he wrote so well about cruelty because he recognized it in himself.

In mid-morning Koestler rang to say he would soon arrive so that Jane and I could read aloud parts of the proofs of his newest book, *The Trail of the Dinosaur*; he wanted to discuss the copy editor's queries. Jane withdrew to her bedroom. He had the kind of throbbing hangover that makes someone sit rigidly upright, ultra-sensitive to all sounds. I bet his eyeballs were buzzing. He detested Jane's Siamese cat, Fur, and the clever creature knew it: crouching close to his chair, she let out a series of guttural yowls while staring at him; he clutched his forehead. When I finished reading, he asked what he owed me. Surprised, I hesitated. Sternly he said I should *never* work for free. Then suddenly he smiled: "I gave you a pound last night! *That* is your payment."

Thereafter he hardly ever came to Blomfield Road; he had mailed Jane a check for the abortion. But several weeks later we were all due at a summer party in Bayswater, and Jane asked Colin and me to keep an eye on him—in case he started to chase other women, as he often did. We felt burdened by that request, although Colin—who had been absent during the turmoil of the last month—said Koestler was "a nice little man" and that he hoped Jane would marry him "so I can drive his MG." At the party he waved tipsily at us across the room; "Well, children, having a good time?" Then he made a pass at the host's plump young nanny, and we felt liberated from our assignment. (Eventually he and Jane would become friends; amiable relations would last throughout his lifetime.)

My husband-to-be was at that party in a sprawling house— once the home of Peter Pan's creator, J. M. Barrie—although we didn't meet. Two and a half years later our wedding reception would take place there: unforeseen nuptials were going to derail a rapturous love affair which should never have lunged into marriage. Places ought to possess the gift of prophecy: I should have felt a tremor from the future in that living room filled with strangers I would often see again: my husband's friends. But fate stayed mum on the Koestler evening as I stood nervously upright in my flowered summer frock and listened to a Harry Belafonte record:

> I'm sad to say
> I'm on my way,
> Won't be back
> For many a day . . .

It was the first time I'd heard "Kingston Town" and I would hum it while I took skiing lessons during my honeymoon in the French Alps.

Some years before Koestler's dive at the nanny, Cyril Connolly wrote to Edmund Wilson, "Like everyone who talks of ethics all day long one could not trust [Koestler] half an hour with one's wife, one's best friend, one's manuscripts, or one's wine merchant. . . . He burns with the envious paranoic hunger of the Central European ant-heap, he despises everybody and can't conceal the fact when he is drunk." Wilson replied, "He carries obnoxiousness to a point where you realize that nobody can be as bad as that—if he was, he wouldn't behave so."

I didn't run into Koestler again until three years later, when he exclaimed, "Why Nora, how you've grown!" It was true; I'd grown an inch when I was twenty-four. But I wished to be suave and worldly with him, and his remark reduced me to the status of a child. I made a joke about being homesick for New York, saying that was my expatriate inch, while he shook his head at my frivolity and zoomed into an elaborate theory about hormones and adult growth. He was jovial yet earnest, eloquent, benign—and I couldn't manage to dislike him, although I thought I should. I could even like him because I'd never been his target. With my new inch and my highest heels I towered over him, the big head nodded as he talked, and I felt oddly secure because I knew that no one like him would ever be central to my life.

In March 1983 the dead bodies of Arthur and Cynthia Koestler were found in the living room on Montpelier Square. Seated in an armchair he held a glass of brandy; she lay on a sofa, half a glass of whisky and a jar of honey on a nearby table. They had swallowed enormous doses of barbiturates in the honey.

At seventy-seven Koestler had advanced Parkinson's disease and leukemia; his doctor had recently found that the cancer was spreading. His friends weren't startled by his suicide. As vice president of the Voluntary Euthanasia Society, he had fought as fiercely for the right of the terminally ill to die—he called it "self-deliverance"—as he had battled capital punishment in the Fifties. (He and the publisher Victor Gollancz had launched the campaign against hanging that finally resulted in its abolition.) No one, he said, was entitled to kill another person—and everyone was entitled to kill himself when an incurable disease worsened.

Koestler's friends thought he didn't fear death; although he belonged to no orthodox religion, he'd been attracted to mysticism since the late Forties. (I never heard him talk about it. But his absorption in the paranormal perplexed—and alienated—many of his former colleagues in science and politics.) He felt that dying could mean "merging into cosmic consciousness." In a suicide note written a year before his death, he said he had "some timid hopes for a depersonalized after-life"—not as a coherent soul, but existing "beyond the confines of space, time, and matter and beyond the limits of our comprehension."

Over the years he had written about an "oceanic feeling" which had sustained him at dire moments (as in his cell in Seville): a sense that "I was floating on my back in a river of peace, under bridges of silence"—and that he "had ceased to exist," having reached a point of "absolute catharsis." Although Koestler's friend George Mikes, the Hungarian writer, couldn't share Koestler's transcendental views, he respectfully quoted him on "the process of dying . . . 'the flow of a river into the ocean.'" The river, mingling with the sea, catches the light, and Koestler "hoped, vaguely, that he might leave some trace of having lived, a sparkle on a river, a fragrance, or a light."

Both he and his wife had been suicidal long before they expired. But her death—she was in fine health at fifty-five—shocked the Koestlers' intimates. To the statement he wrote just before they died, she added only a few words: "I cannot live without Arthur, despite certain inner resources." There were many tributes to her devotion. His male friends claimed that she had thrived on self-sacrifice, and his literary executor stressed that she was "happy" as "wife-secretary-cook-housekeeper-companion." At least once she had signed a letter to Koestler as "your slavey." But in their joint unfinished memoir, written several years before they planned to kill themselves, they left some clues to her vulnerability. He wrote, "I have always picked one type: beautiful Cinderellas . . . prone to be subdued by bullying."

She wrote, "I wish Arthur were not so infectious. He has also infected me with his moods—his depressions and melancholias."

Speculating about the suicides with the writer Caroline Blackwood, who'd known him well, I said I was skeptical about the myth that Cynthia Koestler had died for love. After all, their close friends were quite sure that, even a few days before the fatal doses, she had not been expecting to die. Caroline reminded me about Koestler's frantic nagging and browbeating, the domestic terrorism I'd seen in his days with Jane Howard. What if there had never been what the press called "a suicide pact?" Maybe, Caroline said, he had demanded that his wife die with him, she had recoiled, wanting to go on living, and he'd declared that he would not commit suicide on his own: if she didn't join him, she would have to watch him suffer hideously as cancer and Parkinson's progressed—and she would know that his agonies were _all her fault_. His torments would become hers, with additional lashings of guilt. Caroline and I saw Cynthia Koestler as cornered and choiceless: bested by a man who had escaped death so often that he would not let it take him at random. Instead, death was invited into the house where I had hovered in the darkness on the doorstep—so that Koestler could control it.

# II.

My gypsy life took me to a small bleak basement in Bourne Street, just on the edge of Chelsea, where I wrote synopses of fourth-rate thrillers and pulsating romances for the London bureau of MGM—I had to use paper with ARS GRATIA ARTIS engraved above the lion's head—started to review French and American books for the *New Statesman* (then Britain's leading weekly), read fiction for the publishing firm Eyre and Spottiswoode, and wrote essays and reviews for *The Twentieth Century,* a wonderfully eclectic monthly subtitled "Formerly the Nineteenth Century and After." Sometimes the sight of feet trudging past the basement window was disheartening, and I remembered "from whose bourns no traveler returns" as well as Hamlet's image of death as an unknown country.

Aiming to blot out the past—mainly my parents' tremendous troubles with one another—refusing to think about the future, I was very good at living in the present, certain that all sorts of surprises awaited me. I had almost no confidence in myself, I was shy. But I was elated by discovering my national identity: England was teaching me how American I was and prompting me to immerse myself in Fitzgerald and Hemingway as I never

had before. In the midst of *The Great Gatsby* I would emerge
from my dark basement exhilarated by feeling that Americans
can do anything they want to, are free to follow any path in the
world. My English contemporaries didn't show much appetite
for freedom: I thought Oxford and Cambridge (which I loathed
because of the compulsory small talk) were giving lessons in lim-
itations. But as I hastened through Sloane Square and along the
King's Road, past the gleaming espresso bars and the Victorian
pubs, buying the cheapest eggs or a bunch of mimosa, peering at
the orange and yellow posters for new plays at the Royal Court
Theatre or at Mary Quant's bright dresses in the window of
Bazaar, I felt that anything was possible: if not in this city or on
this street, then over the horizon or in another country.

Since the age of fifteen I'd usually been part of a couple, falling
for one young man after another. Now I was slowly separating
from the boyfriend who had been at Oxford. We lived together
part-time in a glum furnished flat in Woodfall Street, near the
King's Road; in the bathroom there was a framed poster of a pink
elephant getting drunk on champagne: bubbles popped out of
its ears and the caption was PICKLES YOU TINK. We kept quarreling—about the price of theater tickets (he wanted balcony
seats, I didn't), about when to have sex, about the symbolism in
Conrad's *Heart of Darkness*, about my wearing the wrong shoes
for country walks—and I began to wonder if I was an impossible
person, or if he was. Then we parted quite sadly when he went
into the American Army. Not being in love with anyone—
although I longed to be—left me more open, more responsive to
strangers and my surroundings than I might have been if my
emotions had centered on one man. Amid the plane trees and al-
mond blossoms of Chelsea, where the streets teemed with men in
duffle coats and young women in black stockings, I was tasting
the unforeseen rewards of being on one's own.

Koestler was right: London was an international city. Looking
for more work I roamed among groups that barely overlapped:

Anglophobe Parisians whose jobs in advertising tied them to London, which they despised except for Harrods; British editors and writers who fed Fleet Street, complaining about the power of the press while wielding it; blacklisted American film-makers. I kept crossing and recrossing frontiers, good exercise for a beginning writer.

Headlines reported that the anti-Communist crusade was in full swing in my country. But no one I knew in London seemed to regard the small British Commmunist Party as a threat, not even after Guy Burgess and Donald Maclean, the diplomats who had disappeared in 1951, surfaced in Moscow in 1956. The ensuing uproar about spies concentrated on how the Oxbridge establishment had promoted and protected two alcoholic Communists with privileged backgrounds and connections (public school and Cambridge). The steaming embarrassment of the old-boy network seemed as intense as the alarm over secrets stolen from the Foreign Office and the British Embassy in Washington. The fact that Burgess was gay and Maclean bisexual appeared to have furnished further protection: among gentlemen it would have been boorish to penalize an associate for homosexuality. (In the Twenties and Thirties some graduates of elite English schools had seen homosexuality as a form of youthful revolt, an amusing way of horrifying older generations.)

Burgess used to breakfast on brandy, port, and benzedrine, Maclean got into fights and frenzies in nightclubs; and both were famous for flaming indiscretions. It was said that their behavior proved they couldn't be spies, while their patrons had still seen each man as "one of us," part of the inner circle of the governing classes. (Early on neither Winston Churchill nor Anthony Eden was interested in unraveling the case.) The Under-Secretary of State pronounced Maclean "almost too good to be true" shortly after a series of drunken public freak-outs in Cairo. The government tried to suppress the scandal in what historians have called an official conspiracy of silence, which only animated Fleet

Street; the press blamed the security services and the Foreign Office for incompetence rather than scourging the Communist Party. (The aftershocks would be even bigger when Kim Philby, once head of the Soviet section of the British Secret Service and long under suspicion, was revealed as a master spy in 1963. He was much more dangerous than Burgess and Maclean; he had sent dozens to their deaths in Albania and had arranged the executions of agents he'd worked with or recruited—by fingering them to the Russians.) After Burgess and Maclean defected, many gay men were arrested and prosecuted in a campaign against "ghouls of perverted sex," as the romance novelist Barbara Cartland called them. In the mid-Fifties, homosexuality was still a criminal offense, despite a lenient public.

As I became acquainted with parts of the British intelligentsia—mainly through the *New Statesman* and its contributors who also wrote for *The Observer* and *The Manchester Guardian* or for the BBC—I thought that few believed in progress, despite the amenities of the welfare state and the prosperity of the late Fifties. Here I'm speaking of people in their thirties and forties who had fought the Nazis or lived through the Blitz; now they aimed to enjoy themselves. More than ten years after the war had ended, when gloomy postwar austerity had been replaced by a happy hedonism, Londoners—including many with modest salaries—were buying clothes and cars, painting their war-grimed houses, planting flowers in window boxes, crowding into new French and Italian restaurants, winging off for Mediterranean holidays while the press celebrated a "consumer boom."

In Britain at that time there wasn't a popular culture that attracted people over twenty or thirty. Of course jazz spanned the generations. But I'm talking about an era shortly before the Beatles and the Rolling Stones, before acid and widely smoked grass, polyester, miniskirts, and psychedelia. The young weren't yet setting the styles for dress and dancing. Still, there was a gaiety, an ebullience, that shone through the smog; some whose own youth had been dominated by the war seemed livelier and younger than their juniors.

But those I knew did not appear to expect society to advance or international relations to improve. Priding themselves on pragmatism, they seemed uninterested in ideology, although most did believe in socialism with a small *s*. Perhaps they thought it could not be further developed, that it had already changed society as much as was possible. Most seemed to be skeptics rather than cynics, and they detested whatever they thought pretentious. Vigorous critics of their milieu, they applauded the mutinous plays of John Osborne and relished the defiant comedies of Kingsley Amis and John Wain. They also loved ragtime, bebop, and Dixieland, and American movies: *Bad Day at Black Rock* was a particular favorite.

At the height of his enthusiasm for the theater of rebellion, Kenneth Tynan, that elegant iconoclast, stated that it would be necessary to re-create the entire social structure. But iconoclasm was already pivotal to the period's artistic life, and left-wingers who criticized the welfare state seemed to have no blueprint for a replacement. At any rate the arts—especially the theater—were flourishing in the second half of the Fifties. There was a strenuous battle against censorship, but it was won in a few years. Dwelling in a left-liberal culture whose publications challenged almost every aspect of the norm, writers could take their freedom of expression for granted while lampooning the providers of that freedom.

The campaigns against capital punishment and nuclear weapons attracted more supporters each year, uniting individuals of otherwise different views. But this was seen less as an emblem of progress than as a sign of a rational society. It was *unreasonable* to hang people or to risk nuclear accidents or even war, no sensible person could disagree. Over the years, passion did surge through the Campaign for Nuclear Disarmament, spurred by the proliferation of weapons, and the colossal sit-ins in Trafalgar Square grew even larger. The paradoxical nature of many British intellectuals was conspicuous as they became more passionate while insisting they they were governed by reason. V. S. Pritchett had the best term for them: "headlong rationalists."

Skilled reasoners also displayed a scorn for religion ("God-bothering") and metaphysics. This was plainly a post-Christian decade; the majority of the writers I knew were keen atheists. While most of the novels of Graham Greene and Evelyn Waugh were venerated as classics, it seemed as though many English readers overlooked the authors' faith. And there was no respect for any kind of ambivalence: I kept hearing "What *exactly* do you mean?" (or sometimes "What exactly do you mean by *that*?"). The question was a hangover from Bloomsbury, as I later learned from Leonard Woolf's autobiography. He recalled the influence of the philosopher G. E. Moore on his friends and students at Trinity College, Cambridge, where he instilled them with "his peculiar passion for truth, for clarity, and common sense," along with what Maynard Keynes defined as "the duty to know *exactly* what one means and feels." The intention was Socratic, the goal was to banish "humbug" and "irrelevant extraneous matter," and Moore's disciples were taught "that one should not say anything unless it was both true and worth saying." But Woolf also remembered a ghastly small dinner party in the late Twenties when Virginia Woolf asked a novelist, "What do you mean by the Holy Ghost?" and he angrily replied, "I did not say 'Holy Ghost,' I said 'the whole coast.'" Some thirty years afterward, the maddening question could be employed as a rebuke to someone whose ideas were still evolving.

Despite the stress on reason, most of my London acquaintances—married or not—were in the midst of turbulent love affairs. As partners kept splitting and recombining, some said it was an era of flux, as though their private lives mirrored the changes that were occurring all around them. Many Tories as well as Socialists thought the class system was dissolving, which was partly true—it was loosening—and partly an illusion, because many seemed to aspire to social superiority.

Those who declared that the monarchy should be abolished, or at least pensioned off—because the bonehead royals were a terrific expense to the taxpayers and set such a mediocre example to the populace—admitted that many citizens cherished the throne as a symbol of continuity. And middle-class Britons were probably irked by John Osborne's definition of the Royal family: "the gold filling in a mouthful of decay." But whenever I was told that working people revered their Queen, I recalled how a blue-collar audience had howled with helpless laughter at a newsreel of Her Majesty making the first direct call between London and Edinburgh. As she slowly poked her index finger into the holes of a rotary phone, breathing hard and frowning with effort, it was plain that she'd rarely dialed before, perhaps never. Prince Philip looked horribly embarrassed. As the film cut to the Lord Mayor of Edinburgh standing stiffly in his ceremonial robes and staring at an instrument that hadn't yet rung, the spectators whooped and hollered. When at last she completed the call and spoke in piercing tones—"*Hullo* . . . this is . . . the *Queen speaking*," they were almost on the floor, roaring more loudly than they had at the Marx Brothers before the newsreel. Afterward, when people of all ages were still snorting and chuckling, I saw that Elizabeth II had outdistanced *Duck Soup*.

Although I liked London, I hugely missed New York and was very glad to spend time with itinerant Americans, mostly friends of my parents. They fed me well while I clamored for news of my city: what plays had opened? How did Third Avenue look without the El? and they seemed amused by my greed for transatlantic bulletins.

Always a fast walker, I still had to exert myself to keep pace

with the brisk waddle of A. J. Liebling as he strode across St.
James's Street toward a sublime meal in one of his favorite
London restaurants such as Jack's Club in Orange Street or
Wiltons. Perhaps he speeded up when the destination meant eating. (His wartime friends swore that he was the only person
who'd managed to get gout from rich feeding in black-market
bistros during during the Blitz.) "Eat more," he used to croak,
"have more," as I dove into platters of cold poached salmon or
tournedos or skate in black butter. He deplored the popular fiction that the young don't need to eat—later he would be horrified to hear that the novelist Jean Stafford had fed herself
mustard sandwiches when dining alone—and he used to send
me cans of Swiss fondue and lush soups from Fortnum & Mason:
grouse and cock-a-leekie, lobster bisque and sorrel soup, which
arrived like CARE packages in my Bourne Street basement.

Liebling's silences were legendary: his admirers often alluded
to the interview techniques that served him so well: he would un-
nerve his subjects by staring at them but asking almost nothing,
so that they soon began to babble, revealing far more than they'd
intended but gaining little response from the impassive New
York Buddha's face. As he wrote toward the end of his life, "A
good reporter, if he chooses the right approach, can understand a
cat or an Arab. The choice is the problem, and if he chooses
wrong, he will come away scratched or baffled. (There is a different approach to every cat and every Arab.)" Convinced that
"the worst thing an interviewer can do is talk a lot about himself," he was contemptuous of writers "who go out and impress
their powerful personalities on their subject and then come back
and make up what they think he would have said if he had had a
chance to say anything." He was pleased with his preparation for
a profile of the jockey Eddie Arcaro. "The first question I asked
was, 'How many holes longer do you keep your left stirrup than
your right?' Most jockeys on American tracks ride longer on
their left side. That started him talking easily and after an hour,

during which I had put in about twelve words, he said, 'I can see you've been around riders a lot.' I had, but only during the week before I was to meet him."

Liebling was a fairly speechless figure in the halls of *The New Yorker,* nodding affably at colleagues as he passed them but rarely bothering to waste his words on greetings. Maybe that muteness saved his energies for writing. (Thurber, who had a few fantasies about physiques and productivity, said to me, "Liebling is the only fast-writing fat man I know.") Yet the silence may also have sprung from shyness. Balanced against the gleeful arrogance about his work and his success, there was a diffidence that didn't show in print. And he was prone to depressions, which probably silenced him too.

But in England—when he was separated from his second wife but had not yet met Jean Stafford—he astounded his New York acquaintances with his sudden volubility. No Anglophile, he was eager to see Americans in London. There he became loquacious as well as scribacious, talking freely about his writing, his life, his excursions all over the world. He was also very sympathetic to beginners: recalling early struggles and meager earnings, he shared recollections of his own appprenticeship. (Elsewhere he observed that the Pulitzer School of Journalism at Columbia, which he had attended after being expelled from Dartmouth for failing to go to chapel, "had all the intellectual status of a training school for future employees of the A.&P.") And he often talked about "lucky encounters," meaning many of the persons and adventures that seemed to well up in his life by chance. But he wasn't being modest when he spoke of chance: he stressed that almost any kind of writer should perpetually expose himself to the surprises which will yield his meatiest material, and that one must nurture the instinct for being in the right place at the right time, whether on a noontime walk up Piccadilly or heading for a foreign country just before history erupts.

Voluptuously proud of his achievements—I asked what I

should read about the fall of France, which engrossed me at the time: "I wrote the best," he muttered happily between mouthfuls of cassoulet, "the best"—he also seemed to identify with those who were just starting out. (He mocked, as he had in print, his American contemporaries in France: some earnestly tried to learn painting, but nobody tried "to learn how to write, because in the Twenties that was supposed to come naturally, like falling off a bar stool.") He told me about being in Paris at twenty-three during an irresolute period when he felt his life hinged on an impossible decision. He was writing a novel about a twenty-three-year-old in Paris whose future hung upon an insoluble choice. Finally the character caught up with Liebling's own day-to-day existence: he'd reached the very afternoon that he was writing about. Heaving with laughter at his youthful frustrations some thirty years afterward, he had to put down his fork and wipe his eyes before he could focus on his guinea hen.

From London he went several times to France, retracing his war correspondent's route through Normandy and remembering his student days at the Sorbonne. *Normandy Revisited,* one of his finest books, blended wartime memories with glimpses of Paris in the Twenties, both seen from the perspective of the mid-Fifties: history mingled with spurts of autobiography. Master of the Proustian flashback, he was transported to the past by odors and sights and tastes: pollen from mulberry trees, a sip of muscadet, the flavor of Seckel pears or fresh herring. He even allowed free association to take him back to his New York childhood: at low tide the mud flats surrounding Mont-Saint-Michel smelled like Jamaica Bay, where he'd dug clams as a small boy.

On D-day, accompanying the American Army's First Division across the Channel, he was on a landing craft that was transferring wounded men in elevated wire baskets to a hospital ship, when a quart of blood drenched his upturned face and a shell hit a case of condensed milk on the deck, which was soon awash with blood and milk. The day of the liberation of Paris was "one of the happiest of my life": an old Chevrolet bore him through the joyful streets until he reached the café where he'd toasted the arrival of Charles Lindbergh's plane in Paris in 1927. The layers of Liebling's experiences—before, during, and after the war—enlarge a reader's understanding of France throughout the tragedies and comic subplots of its history. My future husband—an Englishman eight years my senior—said it seemed very odd to him that the war, which had been consequential to his life, had hardly touched mine. So I would quote Liebling to show that I wasn't entirely ignorant.

In the fall of 1956 Liebling was researching a piece on the Crazy Gang, an elderly British foursome of music-hall comedians whom he loved. Israel, Britain, and France invaded Egypt because President Gamal Abdel Nasser had nationalized the Suez Canal. Since Liebling couldn't resist a war, he cabled *The New Yorker* that he must go to Egypt at once. He was outraged when the editor William Shawn told him that he should stick with the Crazy Gang and that the Suez crisis would be analyzed by Janet Flanner and Mollie Panter-Downes, the magazine's Paris and London correspondents. He was very fond of the latter, but he regarded all wars as his personal territory and he kept repeating that it was incredible that Shawn should be so blind as to waste a war without some matchless Liebling coverage. Soon he was in what a friend of his had called "a nugly mood," which probably paralleled his distress just before the outbreak of World War II, when he pined to be in France "to share the fight or the risk" but feared he wouldn't have the opportunity to do so.

In London he fumed further during those weeks when British taxi drivers made wisecracks about the "sixpence for Nasser": the increase on their meters due to the shortage of oil and gas that resulted from the blocking of the Suez Canal. Headlines such as LET THE CRY BABIES HOWL! IT'S *GREAT* BRITAIN AGAIN had already burst forth in *The Daily Sketch*, and many English citizens seemed to assume that Nasser could be easily defeated.

While most of my London friends were violently opposed to the government's action, they found themselves battling intimates and relatives with a vehemence that nearly shattered some relationships: the passions reached a pitch that I didn't witness again until Vietnam. Liebling wrote to Jean Stafford, his wife-to-be, that the British "were split as never since the Spanish [Civil] War and Munich."

At the height of Liebling's disgruntlement, I went with him to the large gathering on November 6 sponsored by the Labour Party at the Albert Hall, where some seven thousand had massed to denounce the war policy of Prime Minister Anthony Eden and the Tories. (Liebling wrote afterward that the pro-war Tories were "dizzied by memories of old pleasures, like sentimental Southerners who want one more slave to beat just for old times' sake.") The protesters chanted "Eden must go!" But most were jubilant because the cease-fire had been announced a couple of hours before the rally; now they were celebrating their belief that they were responsible for forcing the government to reverse its position. (They couldn't have known that pressure from Washington and a run on sterling contributed to that retreat: British politicians lied on both counts.) That week Liebling was equally absorbed in the Hungarian uprising against the Russians and in the American election. In that crowd of merry British Socialists he was downcast, musing on the bloodshed in Budapest—the Soviet troops had returned there on November 3—and the predictable defeat of Adlai Stevenson, which occurred that very night. But he remarked that it was nice to be among people who could feel victorious about anything. (Admiring Stevenson, he had written about the reporter Alva Johnson, who believed that "stupid presidents are best," "It is a pity he did not live to see Eisenhower.")

Liebling did get to Egypt after the fighting, arriving there in late November, and came back full of jokes about traveling to inspect the Suez Canal in a taxi. Although he'd been disgusted

by the British invasion and appalled by most of the results of
Britain's seventy-two-year occupation of Egypt, he mumbled
with distinct shame to the *New Yorker* writer Emily Hahn that
he hadn't liked the Egyptians as much as he'd expected to.
Filtering through his *New Yorker* dispatches from Egypt was a
reluctant distaste for the ugliness of Cairo as well as an impatience with "the ingrained Egyptian fear and suspicion of the
West"—even though he felt the latter was absolutely justified.
He was extremely disturbed by the probable expulsion of the
Egyptian Jews holding French or British passports, the persecu-
tion of Jews who were alleged to have "worked against the national security in favor of Israel or Britain or France," and the
future of stateless Jews who had no passports at all.

Despising Eden, who was known for instability and a volcanic
temper, Liebling rocked with laughter a couple of years later
when I described the pre-Suez experiences of an English official
I knew at the UN; he had piloted Eden around when he came to
New York in 1955 to address the members of the Security Council. Beforehand Eden was very chummy in the elevator, where he
kept flinging his arm around the younger man's shoulders. Then
Eden made a maundering speech, which was followed by a question period. Gravely offended by the first questioner's disdain for
his authority, Eden left the meeting. Afterward the atmosphere
in the descending elevator was glacial. By chance the pair journeyed downward with the same cheerful black elevator operator
who'd taken them to their destination. Impressed by the frosty
silence, she asked, "What's the matter? You boys had a fight or
something?" Liebling made me tell him that story several times
in subsequent years; he said he would have given anything to
have been in that elevator: it was his kind of material.

Danger seemed to dodge him and he appeared to be oblivious
to it. He had an unshakable placidity, which probably stayed in-
tact—despite inevitable moments of alarm—as he followed the
First Infantry Division across North Africa during World War

II, dwelling amid Messerschmitts and minefields, and then traveled with the artillery during the 1944 offensive in Normandy, moving through orchards full of snipers, often in company with combat patrols. Earlier he had sailed through the realms of enemy submarines on the North Atlantic, endured the air raids of several countries, and had sprinted through shellfire with the reflection that "It is plausible that the basis of many gestures of self-preservation is simply superstition. The man involved feels that if he does not show solicitude for his own skin he will invite the retaliation of a dark power."

One night in London, the photographer Walker Evans—my parents' contemporary and my friend—and I were dining at Wiltons when Graham Greene walked in with a scarred, seedy little man in a shiny jacket who appeared to have crawled out of the pages of *Brighton Rock*. Evans immediately recognized Greene: the austere face of the dust jackets looked just as formidable leaning over a menu. I had read most of Greene's novels to date, each one quickening my appetite for the next. My favorites were *England Made Me*, *Brighton Rock*, *The Ministry of Fear*, and *The Heart of the Matter*, all such different ballads of betrayal. (As a non-Christian, I was uncomfortable with *The Power and the Glory* and *The End of the Affair*.) Soon after Evans and I had ordered our grilled soles, Liebling rolled into the small restaurant to treat himself to a glorious solitary meal.

Two months before, *The New Yorker* had published his long and ferociously funny attack on Greene's *Quiet American*. Although the review was certainly unfair, it was hilarious reading. Liebling argued that the nationalities of the hard-bitten, worldly English narrator and the naive American had been reversed: the Englishman was a "mock-up" of a Hemingway/Bogart character, while everyone knew that the traits ascribed to the American—sexual gaucherie, a devotion to bad food, lack of imagination, the habit of speaking French abominably—were really endemic to the English. Liebling observed that "a British author snooting American food is like the blind twitting the one-eyed," and he made awful fun of Hemingway/Bogart's addiction to fragile Vietnamese women with birdlike bones who tended to "twitter on his pillow." Declaring that the book was written in "imitation American—brutal brusque sentences tinkling with irony," Liebling indignantly disdained the idea that he didn't live to share: that the American intentions in Vietnam were murderous. The CIA's undercover activities there were not public knowledge at the time; as so often, Greene's fiction was prophetic. In light of Liebling's politics, I'm sure he would have opposed our war against the North Vietnamese had it occurred during his lifetime.

At Wiltons that evening, Liebling sailed blithely into his dinner, unaware that Greene and his companion had frozen on his entrance; they stared furiously at him while whispering with their heads close together. It did look as though a gangland execution were being planned. (Obviously Liebling didn't know Greene by sight.) The charade of deathly enmity persisted throughout several courses, then Liebling joined our table for raspberries and coffee. Now the lethal glares included all three of us. Crowned with the little derby hat he usually wore, Liebling left fairly soon for a conference with the Crazy Gang, still innocent of the lurid glances directed at him. As he had written years before, "The more a man sees of war, the more immediate danger has to be before he starts worrying about it." (I had met Greene once a few months before, but in those days I often tried to be invisible, so he wouldn't have remembered me.)

As Evans and I strolled up St. James's Street, laughing about the extraordinary pantomime we'd seen, we suddenly heard heels hitting the pavement hard behind us. Greene and his sinister friend passed us swiftly, then wheeled around to glower at us.

All the way up that long street they followed or flanked us: one would appear scowling in a lighted doorway, then the other would dart ahead of us, then their footsteps would echo loudly at our backs again. It was my first taste of guilt by association—as though sharing a table with Liebling meant that one shared his loathing of *The Quiet American*. We finally lost our nerve and caught a taxi, wondering if the great novelist was drunk—or if it merely tickled him to tease Americans. Later a friend of Greene's told me that he was an avid practical joker; he liked to play such games, to make others feel ridiculously threatened. (He'd written that in childhood he had enjoyed hide-and-seek in the dark, a diversion "containing the agreeable ingredient of fear.") Intrigue—so splendidly depicted in his books—seemed necessary for his momentary amusement. Briefly he had made us his enemies. Because fear excited him, perhaps he thought it exhilarated others too.

When I told Liebling about it the next day, the bulging eyes widened, then the fat shoulders shook. Between guffaws he gasped that he'd heard that Greene was angered by his review, but he had never realized that a critic could drive a writer to parody his own characters. Due to his passion for accents and inflections, he regretted that no one had heard the voice of Greene's intimidating guest. While I maintained that the man looked like a hood, Liebling fantasized that he was really a writer, maybe even a poet, and quoted the thesis of his friend Charles Boxer, historian of Portuguese and Dutch colonial empires; "Show me a poet and I'll show you a shit."

From Tunisia I received a postcard: "Here I am in Carthage but no Dido," signed Aeneas J. Liebling. Lonely in London until he encountered Jean Stafford, he hurled himself impulsively at a number of women: the suddenness of the onslaught in the taxi or on the banquette caught most by surprise. Yet he also hoped for a renewal of his marriage. He told me that his wife had asked for six months' separation to "think about" resuming their life together. Then, when he returned to New York to see her, she urged him to go away for another six months while she "thought about" it further. He tried to make a joke of this, but as he talked it wasn't funny at all. So he pursued women with a mingling of recklessness and reserve: the abrupt lunge of a man who rather expects to be rejected. Once he made a pass at a very young Englishwoman whose parents were his old friends. She recoiled with some astonishment, since she'd known him all her life and thought of him as a venerable, cozy uncle. (He was fifty-three at the time but looked much older.) Fearing that she'd hurt his feelings, she began to apologize for her involuntary squawk when he cut her short with a pat on the back and rumbled, "Well, as they say in racing, they can't roll you off the track for trying." My response to the lunges was a quick daughterly hug, as though I'd misunderstood him—the result was a swift withdrawal, which preserved dignity on both sides.

Deeply admiring of Jean Stafford's writing, he kept joyfully exclaiming, "It's got balls" right after they met in London. A few years later, when they were married and we were all back in New York, he told me he would like to see her on the same schedule Willy had imposed on the young Colette, and that he wanted her to spend the summer writing a flock of stories and novellas. He complained that she was giving too much time to decorating their home, and that a writer of such unique talents shouldn't waste her mind on slipcovers. "*Slip*covers," he repeated indignantly, shaking his head. He was the only husband I've seen perturbed by his wife's allegiance to housework.

He enjoyed gathering gifts for her: marvelous pieces of antique jewelry emerged from his pockets after he'd been abroad. One day at lunch, while I was examining the earrings and the necklace he had pushed across the table with one finger, he produced a delicate eighteenth-century enamel brooch: on its painted oval, Jacob wrestles with the angel. I handed it back to him, but the finger slowly worked it across the table again and he muttered that it was for me. He'd decided that the angel was a writer and that Jacob was an editor: in this tiny version, the angel was sure to win the struggle. He advised me to always give editors a hard time: "And never spoil them!" (Nevertheless he was mellower in the late Fifties than he had been a decade earlier, when he had castigated editors who couldn't write themselves: "The reign of these non-writers makes our newspapers read like the food in *The New York Times* cafeteria tastes. It is as if, in football, only bad players were allowed to become coaches. Indifference to language thus becomes hierarchized.") He added that he hoped I would some day make as much "trouble" for editors as he had, and I promised I would try. He also warned me, "Never be anyone's protégé," and in a world of little cliques and jealousies I sensed that was good advice and I followed it.

Thereafter I wore the brooch when I was interviewed by new editors, wondering if they'd heard the Liebling dictum that "freedom of the press is guaranteed only to those who own one," or that the press is "the weak slat under the bed of democracy." Yet in middle age he still had enough confidence in his colleagues to write that "newspapermen as a class have a yearning for truth as involuntary as a hophead's addiction for junk . . . A few newspapermen lie to get on in the world, but it outrages them, too, and I never knew a dishonest journalist who wasn't patently an unhappy bastard."

Happiness was not conspicuous in Fleet Street, where the wine bar called El Vino was known as "that graveyard of talent." Probably there were more inventions there than in our Times Square, though I doubt if that disturbed the fabricators. And the *New Statesman* editors I knew didn't seem upset by factual errors that would have mortified most American writers; as furious letters of correction flooded the magazine, the guilty person would cheerfully reply, "Please excuse that slip of the pen" or "I have just realized—too late for correction . . . "

I wrote about this to my father, a fiend for accuracy, and he answered that among British newspapers "there seems to be a tradition of letting fakery slide through unchallenged." By chance he had been one of four war correspondents at the opening of the 1943 Teheran Conference. Another, an Englishman with the United Press ("a big Fleet Street slob") filed a story alleging that during the conference Stalin became so angry at Marshal Semyon Timoshenko that he broke a bottle of vodka over his head. Timoshenko wasn't even in Teheran, but the story was published "all over Christ's earth." The three other writers were blasted by their editors for missing the story. The Russians were so infuriated that there were broadcasts on Moscow radio that the British were talking secretly with Germany's foreign minister Joachim von Ribbentrop about a separate peace—a total fiction. The American correspondents cornered the UP man and asked what the hell he thought he was doing. He said the official information on the conference was "so frightfully dull" that he was merely trying to liven things up.

From conversations with Liebling, I learned to savor London headlines. When a prostitute was killed by a client, *The Daily Express* announced, DOG SEES HIS MISTRESS MURDERED; the story oozed with titillation for animal lovers: the spiciness of "mistress" was blended with pity for the poor dog in the woman's bedroom. *The Times* seemed to specialize in deadpan absurdity: TWO SCOURGES OF RUGGED UGANDA: RITUAL MURDER AND SOIL EROSION. When the British tested their latest H-bomb, the Beaverbrook papers exulted: BANG! BANG! BANG! While Prince Philip was at a football match in Gibraltar and the Queen went to the races in England, *The Daily Mirror* urged, FLY HOME,

PHILIP!; as the palace denied "a Royal rift," the paper entreated
the Prince to join his wife in order to scotch "rumors of discord
in the Royal Family."

Liebling's offices at home and abroad were stacked with shaky
towers of daily and weekly papers: it looked as though he loved
newsprint as much as a joyously remembered meal of roast
pheasant followed by tripe à la mode de Caen, beefsteaks and
soufflé potatoes, goat cheese in ashes, and baked apples with cores
of jelly. Propelled by "historical curiosity," he called himself "a
chronic, recidivist reporter." I wish he had lived long enough to
revel in Watergate, to luxuriate in each Nixon tape as though it
were a gourmet feast, along with the host of characters who
would have rewarded his fascination with minor crooks whose
only fame sprang from disgrace. Liebling's affection for New
York lowlife—at the racetrack, among prizefighters and wrest-
lers, amid conmen, along Broadway—might have generated
sympathy for Nixon's staff, perhaps even for the sullied President
himself.

In those years of Britain's battles with the Mau Mau in Kenya,
Churchill's retirement amid rumors of his senility, guerilla warfare in Cyprus (still under British rule), Suez, Commander Lionel
Crabb, the frogman who disappeared after the Secret Service sent
him to spy on a Russian cruiser in Portsmouth Harbour, Teddy
Boys—young toughs who wore Edwardian clothing and rioted
at showings of *The Blackboard Jungle*—and thick brown and yellow Dickensian fogs (which were banished when soft coal was
outlawed), Liebling appeared to be as much at ease in London as
in New York; while he seemed as American as Grand Central
Station, he had a portable soul. Time spent with Liebling restored
my city to me—while his spirit wandered from one country to
another.

Revisiting a house he'd known in France, he wrote, "I felt I
had come back to one of my homes. (A mobile man has many.
There is, for example, a cabin in a Norwegian tanker that I wake

in often, although I haven't slept there in fourteen years.)" The mobile man was unsentimental and he respected change. His perspective helped me to see that loss doesn't have to be calamitous, as when I read, "Any city may have one period of magnificence like Boston or New Orleans or San Francisco, but it takes a real one to keep renewing itself until the past is perennially forgotten." The idea was new to me—I was mourning the destruction of the Third Avenue El—but I was starting to understand that transformations can be as valuable as births or beginnings, and that they deserve to be celebrated.

# III.

Fat men were my friends. Not lovers—since my father was fat, a paunch turned me off; it was parental, too close to home. Yet I was comfortable with paternal males of my father's generation. From a fat man I expected humor and generosity, eloquence (spoken or written), and surprises—which answered my taste for the unpredictable. I didn't have to look for those portly figures: they found me almost as soon as I went abroad.

Liebling was the first, then came John Davenport, the British literary critic, aesthete, editor, and former heavyweight boxer who didn't discourage the legends that mounted in his wake: he seemed both amused and nourished by them. It was said that T. S. Eliot had pronounced his poetry most promising when he was a student at Cambridge in the late Twenties. It was repeated —with some awe—that he'd been expelled from the Savage Club for putting a small bishop on the mantelpiece: nettled by some discord in their theologies, Davenport had lifted the little prelate into the air and deposited him above the fireplace, declaring, "You talk like a bloody clock and that's where you belong." (Years afterward I heard that it was the Lord Chancellor who was placed on the mantel of the Savile Club, but who knows?) Others recalled that Davenport hurled tureens of tomato soup over the snowy shirtfronts of clubmen whose perceptions of Proust displeased him. He did take literature into his fists: it was a measure of his passion.

He entered my life as a stranger on the telephone, soon after my first few essays were published—a whispery voice with a base of gravel—"You won't remember me, but I used to play bears with you in Hollywood." Pause. "And I once gave you a bath." (It turned out that he'd known my parents in Beverly Hills during his stint of screenwriting there, when I was three and my father was about to write *Annie Oakley* for Barbara Stanwyck.) Brisk instructions followed: "You'd better meet me at noon in the King's Arms in Sloane Square." But how would I recognize him? He mentioned a very red face, gray hair, immense weight but minimal height: "In short, I look like an overgrown dwarf." Assuming that he was joking, I laughed and said I wouldn't come. "Oh, you'd better," he said airily, "It would be *better* if you did." Peering through the fumes of the murky pub I found him instantly, looking exactly as described. And it was easy to imagine his affinities with Dylan Thomas; Davenport had recently written about his dead friend, adding that they'd seen *Lost Weekend* together: "We emerged from the cinema looking as wan as two fat men could, then burst simultaneously into laughter and a bar."

Myth was his element: a fastidious mind, coupled with a rowdy temperament, embellished an extraordinary life. With Thomas he wrote *The Death of the King's Canary* in 1940 and 1941. Devised as a comic thriller concerning the choice of a new poet laureate, brimming with parodies of Eliot, Auden, Spender, the Sitwells, Siegfried Sassoon, and a host of other luminaries of the Thirties, it was intended as "a sort of serious joke" that would earn the collaborators "some money and enemies." They worked in Davenport's grand house in Gloucestershire in the midst of a house party of writers and musicians—Davenport was an excellent pianist as well as a fine linguist and mimic—and Thomas said "the summer talked itself away." The book wasn't published in England until 1976 because of the British libel laws. The manuscript was incomplete or perhaps never finished; a hundred and forty-five characters surface in the same number of pages, and it's difficult to unscramble them from the surrealist plot. The spoof was not successful, but undoubtedly the writers enjoyed themselves, and Thomas called it "the best of its Kind or Unkind."

Davenport was for a while the lead fiction critic of *The Observer* —V. S. Pritchett wrote to him, "Nobody has so wide a grasp as you or so fine an eye"—and he also wrote frequently for *The Spectator* (where his future obituary would announce that "as a reviewer of contemporary fiction, he had no equal"). His reading outdistanced that of many academics and he seemed to have memorized much of what he'd read. With his friend James Stern, the Irish short-story writer who introduced him to the novels of Patrick White—one of his favorites—Davenport loved to unearth new writers and to circulate their work. (How many underpaid critics exert themselves for strangers?) Years before Karen Blixen's books were widely known, he celebrated her talents. With each discovery he could convince you that it was essential to instantly immerse yourself in a certain book. Having spent a couple of years in the United States, he was rather possessive about American literature, and he kept exhorting his English audience to read Melville (especially *Bartleby*), Faulkner, and Conrad Aiken at a time when they hardly did so. But he didn't care for the later Hemingway: to Stern he wrote, "I cannot abide sentimentality, & the worst, for me, is the 'tough' (soft as Bratwurst) American variety." Of Hemingway he also said, "Poor old silly, couldn't even strangle a rhinoceros with his bare hands."

Detecting the ability of fledglings was one of his many achievements. As an undergraduate at Cambridge, he was a close friend of Malcolm Lowry; in 1932 he advised Lowry to send the manuscript of *Ultramarine* to Chatto and Windus, one of London's

most distinguished publishing houses. In 1936 it was to Davenport that Lowry desperately appealed between bouts of terrify-
ing imprisonment in a Mexican jail. (Lowry wrote to Davenport
that he feared "imminent insanity. . . . This is not the cry of the
boy who cried wolf. It is the wolf itself who cries for help.")
Davenport was also early to recognize Dylan Thomas's gifts.
Both Lowry and Thomas remained Davenport's lifelong friends,
and he hauled them out of some muddy financial swamps. He
was once rather rich but became very poor; in his flusher days he
spent a good deal on sustaining writers and painters.

But above all he gave writers the kind of encouragement that
becomes fuel. From the Thirties to the early Sixties he functioned
as a free-floating editor and teacher: praising and scolding and
demanding the very best from the beginners he wanted to flourish. Hearing him talk was a privilege that delighted many writers—especially a group from the *New Statesman*—as he held
court in Chelsea pubs or in anyone's living room. The critic
Conrad Knickerbocker remembered "his soft, rich voice, reso-
nant beyond breeding, beyond Cambridge, beyond literature, the
once eternal sound of civilization, but also faintly menacing."
Being exposed to his vocabulary was an education for the ear: his
speech intensified your sensitivity to language and bestowed a
heightened awareness of its possibilities. After a dose of Davenport, you were all the more responsive to classical or contemporary prose or to the vivid fluencies of the street. His conversation
made you immediately wish to go home and write. So he gave
you momentum. Unlike many thwarted artists, he wanted others to do what he couldn't often do himself.

Mine was the last generation Davenport helped to nurture. He
would arrive for an unscheduled lunch in my Bourne Street basement, bringing bacon and frozen string beans and books and im-
peratives: "Why don't you eat *this* . . . read *this* . . . write about
*that*." Soon those editorial sessions were part of my London week:
he read my pieces before I submitted them, plucking out passages

that needed polishing but never suggesting any words of his own, instilling a horror of clichés; introduced me to one of the best editors I ever worked with; coached me in coping with another who was prone to peevish disorders. Of the latter he asked eagerly, "Shall I knock him down?" I protested violently. Davenport soon found another excuse, which engrossed the Chelsea shut-ins —writers who scarcely moved muscles that weren't in their jaws—"He was talking such frightful rot about Faulkner that I simply had to knock him out." Of yet another editor I found difficult, he said loftily, "He can't get a cock-stand"—as though impotence was the cause of inept editing.

One day he fussed at the sight of a button dangling from my coat as I was heading for the MGM office; "That looks terrible. Sew it on *now*." No thread. "Oh, *why* don't Americans *ever* have any thread?" he cried, rushing me to Woolworth's. The threadlessness of Americans made me wonder what experience had been recalled: torn flies in Hollywood or burst suspenders? What ravaged jacket or ruined sleeve awoke the memory of a turbulent evening in California? Then he hurried me to the Commercial, his favorite pub on the King's Road, where I sewed while he lectured about the absurdity of the concept of sexual characteristics—"*I* can sew"—and the perversity of those who believed in traditional gender roles.

Writing about friendship, Davenport displayed a trait that charmed his acquaintances: "One doesn't have to be a rebel oneself to appreciate rebellion in others. I have been lucky in knowing so many revolting people: I mean people in revolt from the smugness of conventional society, who were able to be natural and creative and share life, without seizing bits of it and crawling off to devour them in some private hole, like so many crabs in a tank." Was friendship accidental? Probably not: "One bumps into people all over the world whom one seems destined to know." In Kenya he picked wildflowers from the grave of Karen Blixen's dead lover, Denys Finch-Hatton, then brought them to her in Copenhagen. "She takes such links for granted. . . . They are divinely planned, these patterns of friendship, and part of the whole texture of one's life. One does not set out to make friends any more than one sets out to be happy—an impossible enterprise."

Happiness fled from him; his personal life seethed with disasters, though he was proud of his sons and daughters. His first wife divorced him and his second committed suicide. Doubtless he gave both a great deal of pain. And his attitude toward women in general could be patronizing even when it was comic: a friend of mine heard him groan, "Oh all those wonderful women, cunts like cathedrals—*why* do they want to be writers?" But he admired Mary McCarthy's novels before he encountered her in Rome in the spring of 1956. I can vouch for that because he borrowed my American edition of *A Charmed Life* before it was published in England. When I complained about the dullness of the long scene where a character partly based on Edmund Wilson holds forth on Racine's *Berenice*, *Hamlet*, and other classics, Davenport asserted that the lengthy discourse was essential to reveal the workings of the polymath's mind; it was far more effective than if she'd merely stated, "He was brilliant that evening."

Still married to her third husband, McCarthy fell in love with Davenport soon after they met, embarking on what the writer Frances Kiernan called "her one great European romance." Davenport wrote to James Stern, "She made Rome for me. Odd that we should click so firmly. She turned out to be a J. D. fan, which helped at the kick-off. After that it was roses, roses and an occasional Negrone all the way." Later she wrote to Hannah Arendt, "This has all gone very deep, on both sides." Arendt thought the affair could continue for twenty years. But it lasted only until 1957, when he ceased answering McCarthy's letters—

an enigmatic withdrawal—and she was devastated to learn that he'd told many of his London friends about it. Ignoring his own marriage, she had wished for a time to marry him. In great distress she admitted to Arendt, "The truth is, I still care about him, just as much as ever." Feeling that their situation was "hopeless" because of the "publicity" he'd given their liaison, she had an angina attack, the result of "a broken heart." Shortly before her death in 1989 she told one of her future biographers how important and satisfying the affair had been to her.

I should say that he never made a pass at me; after all, he was a member of my extended family. To an old friend he wrote, "What is awful about being fifty is that I am quite unable to feel differently from what I felt when I was sixteen." Some thought him a permanent adolescent, but that very quality was what enabled him to understand so much about those who were half his age or less. Though I didn't confide in him, he seemed to guess what was on my mind, and once he told me not to worry about my life, that I had everything I needed except money. In a faraway rasping voice he added, "Worry about anything in the world, but not about yourself. There's no need." I wrote that down. He also said there were very few things one had to do: if you were broke, then you had to earn; if relatives were ill, you had to arrange for their care. Tilting against the anxieties of the young, he said you didn't have to see people you didn't like, didn't have to give presents you couldn't afford, or to submit politely to unwanted caresses. He was telling me that I was freer than I realized, which was just what I needed to hear at twenty-three.

Davenport liked to remember the cracked and nearly empty swimming pool at my parents' house in Beverly Hills; it held only an inch or two of rainwater and was full of chorusing frogs. "Noisy," he said, "An empty pool of noise. Of course I wouldn't want to strain the metaphor." (He was thinking of Hollywood.) He knew that my family's earnings had since been swallowed by the cost of my mother's mental and physical illnesses. One day I found a mysterious three pounds in my purse after lunching with him. Terribly puzzled I wondered if I'd miscounted my cash. That evening I heard from an infuriated mutual friend that three pounds were missing from her purse right after a morning visit from Davenport. For years I lacked the guts to tell her about my startling little bonus.

Mid-century Chelsea was familiar with the sight of Davenport and Toffee, his vast brown poodle, which padded ahead of him along the King's Road on the end of a short, thick chain—the man leaning back against the tug of the dog's weight. When Davenport's friends sat around him in a Chelsea pub, Toffee usually lay at the feet of whoever was in charge of the conversation (often his owner). But if the speaker lost his lead, the poodle would rise and amble over to the person who had caught the group's attention. Bruised confidence was apparent in the faces of those Toffee abandoned.

Fistiness apart, Davenport had quite a bit in common with Cyril Connolly—bulk and brilliance, elegance of intellect, an obsession with quality, influence on young writers, flab, debts—but he attacked Connolly savagely in the *New Statesman* after an excerpt of a novel appeared in *Encounter*. Possibly Davenport was flogging some flaws he perceived in himself, and it was true that Connolly's literary power was weightier than his own. Davenport used to mock Connolly's particular blend of hedonism and aestheticism and said, "He'd like to be Baudelaire without the syphilis."

The fragment of Connolly's novel was called "Shade Those Laurels"; the Davenport review was titled "Peel Those Medlars." Davenport, who had stimulated so many writers, rebuked Connolly as an inhibiter of talent, a critic who made others fearful of writing what he mightn't approve: "Mr. Connolly is a public benefactor. He has prevented more books from being written than anyone else alive. Apart from Byron, who wrote rather too much, and Oscar Wilde, who wrote more than one realizes, it is unlikely that any literary figure has been so widely discussed by his contemporaries. Is it fear he inspires? Envy? Awe? . . . Verbal wit, a sensuous disposition that could be styled languid if it were less prickly, a mind eclectically furnished and untidy, a day nursery made to accomodate the dead. . . ." Finally Davenport charged that Connolly ruled in a "half-world, where the books are decanted and the bottles read."

Basking in the commotion that followed his essay, Davenport was nonetheless appalled to hear that I hadn't read Connolly's *Enemies of Promise* or *The Unquiet Grave*. A few hours later, battered copies of both fell through my mail slot. Savoring Connolly's best prose, Davenport insisted that it be thoroughly respected—in light of the roasting he gave Connolly's inferior work. James Stern called Davenport "the only living soul who has an unbiased, unbitter eye for the GOODS, who knows at a glance, can tell at one squint of however unjaundiced an eye the gold, the silver, even the copper, from the lead, the mediocre, the meritricious!"

While there's no sin in high standards, the peril of paralysis lurks in impossible ones. Connolly's analysis of those enemies of promise reflects the problems he shared with Davenport and with Desmond MacCarthy, the literary editor of the *New States-man* from 1920 to 1927. MacCarthy, whom Virginia Woolf identified as "the most gifted of us all," was expected to be the successor of Henry James. But, Woolf wrote, "his 'great work' (it may be philosophy or biography now, and is certain to be begun, after a series of long walks, this very spring) only takes shape . . . in that hour between tea and dinner, when so many things appear not merely possible but achieved." The playwright and novelist Enid Bagnold mourned MacCarthy as "a man gone over the edge leaving too little behind," explaining, "It wasn't that Desmond couldn't invent, but he never caught up with his mislaid power to do it." Connolly wrote, "Whom the gods wish to destroy, they first call promising," and he mated promise with guilt: for failing to live up to the anticipations of others. He called it "a crime" not to fulfill one's talents, and perhaps that conviction mirrored the mentality of the Connolly/Davenport literary generation of Oxford and Cambridge. "The sole function of a writer" was to produce a masterpiece and no other task was "of any consequence." Little thought was given to apprenticeship or early experimentation: the promisers were supposed to beget marvels as soon as they started to weave a few words together. But the test of a masterwork was simple: "Would it amuse Horace or Swift or Leopardi? Could it be read to Flaubert?" There was also a fixation on permanence: the artist must "write a book that lasts forever." Later that was modified to "lasting a generation," then to "half a generation," then to "holding good for ten years."

Eventually Connolly wistfully imagined a book that had the hope of "outliving a dog or a car, of surviving the lease of a house or the life of a bottle of champagne." Approaching sixty, he asked, "Has this half century of self-speculation given me nothing to affirm, nothing to render my leaving of the world of more consequence than the mowing of the grass, the shooting of a pheasant, the felling of a tree?" Today while we regret a stalled or curdled talent, no one would consider a writer's block criminal, and when Connolly wrote, "Who would not rather than the best of reviewers be the worst of novelists?" his words echo oddly in contemporary New York, where the most prominent reviewers have much more stature than a fine novelist with a meager audience. But he lacked the drive that made V. S. Pritchett describe writing as "a labor delightful because it is fanatical."

Small wonder that Connolly and Davenport and MacCarthy did not achieve the sublime fiction and poetry expected of them. Besides, all three excelled at conversation, which Connolly defined as "a ceremony of self-wastage." He maintained that "good talkers . . . are miserable; they know that they have betrayed themselves, that they have taken material which should have a life of its own, to dispense it in noises in the air." In this era, television specials might be carpentered around such spell-casters; their spoken words could be valued more than their prose. And Connolly's ghost will have to live with the fact that some of his most memorable paragraphs dwelled on the agony of writing anything at all.

Though it's not possible to be certain of what prevents a talent from thriving, it may have been frustration about writing that caused Davenport to demolish quite a bit of furniture and some sensibilities over the years. The novelist Muriel Spark employed him as a character in *The Bachelors*, where she made him a "mammoth" art critic who was a danger to frail china, prompt to denounce others as "vulgar little fellows" or "common little creatures"—which were Davenport's raspberries to philistines. The fictional art critic lamented his unused talents as a painter, and disappointment was welded to his rage.

I heard about a visit Davenport made toward the end of his life to a country house where friends sought to cheer him when he was very depressed. He slept in or near a room that contained many valuable antique clocks, the collection of a lifetime. When he awoke in the morning he saw that most of them had been shattered: a sea of smashed glass and delicate bits of metal surrounded him. I was told that he had no recollection of destroying them: he couldn't remember those lunges of despair. When he met his hosts at breakfast he gravely informed them that a poltergeist must have been responsible; he stressed that such visitations were frequent in old mansions in that shire. Staring at the wreckage of their choicest possessions they slowly repeated that yes . . . it must have been a poltergeist . . . of course . . . that had to be the explanation. Their no doubt anguished tact conveys the loyalty that many felt to Davenport—whose kindness had nourished his friends for several decades.

After five years in England I moved back to New York and didn't see Davenport until 1965, when I was revisiting London. I ran into him at the theater, during the intermission of James Baldwin's *Blues for Mr. Charlie*. When I began to thank Davenport for those editorial sessions, he beamed and said, "Oh rats. Shut up." I hugged him and he shouted, "More!" Again I tried to express my thanks. "Shut up! More!" He was living fairly near Brighton and I suggested that a friend of his and I might drive down to have a picnic with him. He thought that was a terrible idea: "Can't we have it in the picnic room at Harrods?" Finally he said, "Oh well, we could go and eat hard-boiled eggs on Malcolm Lowry's grave—he'd love it," so I didn't press further. Still, we started to embroider a sampler for him; it was stitched with a quote from Muriel Spark's grandmother: "It is almost never right to make an upset." But he disappeared into his final illness before we could finish it. A host of tributes followed his death, and as his dedication to literature was extolled I wished that there might be a Davenport Award for those rare catalysts and kindlers who abet beginning writers—at what cost to their energies and perhaps to their egos as well.

As an English major at Harvard, grounded mainly in the past, I'd assumed that the world of contemporary British literature would be much like Bloomsbury. How wrong I was. I rapidly learned from the *New Statesman*, *The Observer*, and the BBC that Bloomsbury was in disrepute—even under attack—in modern England. Virginia Woolf was especially unpopular with writers like Kingsley Amis, who were in revolt against the cult of personal relations and experimental prose, elitist assumptions and the complacent isolation of upper-middle-class aesthetes.

Bloomsbury had assailed the class system while perched on its higher rungs, and its members were considered blind to whatever lay outside the cultivation of their sensibilities. After a blast from Amis, who could be awed by the pronouncements of Lytton Strachey or Clive Bell? I was told that the animosity toward Bloomsbury had originated with F. R. Leavis, the powerful Cambridge literary critic and editor of *Scrutiny*, who molded several generations of disciples, especially those from state schools; a couple of those scholarship students became major London editors in the Fifties and Sixties.

In London, where intimates and old foes tended to review one another's books—often ferociously—I found the community of the weeklies and the Sunday papers claustrophobic, quite like Davenport's crabs in a tank. And insults seemed intrinsic to critical essays. Adversarial journalism was practiced with the precision of a martial art: English literary warfare was as cruelly direct as karate, as poisonous as Germany's gases of World War I. But I loved writing for the *New Statesman*—reviewing new American novels, a biography of Walt Whitman, Proust's letters to his mother—and I was honored to appear there. Founded in 1913 by Sidney and Beatrice Webb, Bernard Shaw, and a few fellow Fabians, it merged with *The Nation* in 1931 under the guidance of Keynes. Soon it was known as the "New Staggers and Naggers" or "Stags Mags." (The staggering had pertained to foreign policy in the Thirties, especially in relation to the Soviet Union.) Among its regular contributors were Arnold Bennett, Hilaire Belloc, Julian Huxley, Leonard Woolf, George Orwell, Claud Cockburn, Cyril Connolly, and John Betjeman.

Edward Hyams, the magazine's historian, characterized it as Britain's foremost "organ of dissent," a beacon of inquiry and non-conformity. It had influenced public opinion on anti-fascism in the Thirties and the anti-imperialism that had brought an end to British rule in India and other colonies, also the formation of the welfare state. Some gave it substantial credit for helping to dismantle the Empire and creating the state. Over the decades, the editors hoped to advance the development of Socialism, and the *New Statesman* was on the left of the Labour Party, which it often chastised. (There was no party loyalty, as Labour leaders often complained.) The Campaign for Nuclear Disarmament was initiated by a forceful 1957 article by J. B. Priestley. After Bertrand Russell wrote "An Open Letter to Eisenhower and Khrushchev" about the necessity of averting global war, addressing them as "Most Potent Sirs," the Soviet leader and Secretary of State John Foster Dulles denounced each other in long exchanges in the magazine in 1958.

Essential as it was to British intellectual life for some forty years, the *New Statesman's* greatest strength was literary; the back of the book contained a splendid range of voices and diverse personal styles. (It had a large American readership and was a model for *The New York Review of Books* in its early years.) When I began to write for the magazine, the crown jewel was V. S. Pritchett; to him I owe the word "scribacious," which means fond of writing, as well as dazzling insights on writers from Lady Murasaki, Swift, and Chekhov to Balzac and Kafka and Yeats.

The *New Statesman* displayed an impassioned commitment to literature—indeed a love of literature rarely seen in today's magazines. At that time, the written word seemed almost sacred to London's zealous reading public. An enthusiasm for American writers was expanding while rampant Francophilia (known as "French flu") was ebbing. And British literature of the mid- to late Fifties was flourishing in many directions: books by relatively new writers included William Golding's *Lord of the Flies*, Iris Murdoch's *Under the Net*, Angus Wilson's *Anglo-Saxon Attitudes*, Sybille Bedford's *Legacy*, the first volumes of Doris Lessing's *Children of Violence* series, Muriel Spark's *Memento Mori*, the poetry of Ted Hughes, Sylvia Plath, Stevie Smith, and Thom Gunn. Some had well-deserved success. But although Lawrence Durrell's *Alexandria Quartet* and Colin Wilson's *Outsider* were best-sellers, the lush exoticism of the first and the religiosity of the second weren't likely to appeal to most of the *New Statesman*'s readers.

Kingsley Martin, whom Pritchett called "a restless prophet who contained the fluctuating conscience of the Left," was widely regarded as the most intelligent editor of his generation; he had been in charge of the magazine for nearly thirty years. Now his regime was approaching its end and I met him only a couple of times, once at a vast Silver Wedding reception for the *New Statesman* and *The Nation* held in the ballroom of Londonderry House in Park Lane; a butler bellowed our names as we entered. While corks popped and sardonic toasts were exchanged, I listened to Angus Wilson holding forth on sexual vitality and managed to have a polite conversation with John Raymond, the assistant literary editor, before he grew hostile on champagne.

The office at Great Turnstile was shabby and full of hot plates bubbling with tea or coffee or soup; it all looked rather unprofessional, but it was the most efficient organization I've dealt with. Most of the buildings around the office had been leveled during the Blitz and new ones hadn't yet risen; to deliver a review I walked across a short bridge surrounded by rubble. John Raymond was an estimable editor and an almost impossible person. On his good days Raymond's phone calls after receiving a piece were peppered with keenly specific questions; he pointed out repetitions or noted that the last sentence of my fourth paragraph contradicted the third sentence of the second: "See? *Your* problem, *you* fix it, call me back in fifteen minutes and *don't use an extra word*." From him I was learning how to edit myself. Raymond wrote brilliant essays on Montaigne, Churchill, Colette, Rebecca West, and others, and for four days a week he was ardent in his dedication to "the mag." From Friday through Sunday he was very drunk. Plump, florid, and perspiring, bald at thirty-one, he was unconfident with women, which made him assaultive. The blundering onslaught and the blurted threat—

"You can't review the Poe biography if you don't!"—seemed to invite rejection, which made him cross. But he was probably thankful too: he'd attempted to exercise a droit du seigneur over the contributors, yet didn't have to follow through. Rapidly smoking Gitanes, he scattered ashes everywhere; his colleagues said his office smelled like weed-killer.

A Catholic convert with rather old-fashioned Tory reflexes—apart from his distaste for "the insane cult of Royalty, hatched by a mentally moth-eaten Palace entourage"—he finally allowed booze to wash him out of the *New Statesman* once the wet days outnumbered the sober ones. He was gone by the mid-Sixties, when I became the magazine's New York correspondent. Buoyed by editorial and stylistic freedoms I'd never had in American magazines, my relations with the *New Statesman* were the happiest I'd known with any publication. The office employed a delightful night watchman; on my yearly London visits, if I worked after 9:00 P.M., he would bring me cups of strong purple tea and we'd swap stories and shreds of gossip about the staff.

In the second half of the Fifties, Kingsley Amis, John Wain, Philip Larkin, John Osborne, Alan Sillitoe, John Braine, and their contemporaries most reasonably disliked being called Angry Young Men; the term had been invented for Osborne by a publicist just before *Look Back in Anger* opened at the Royal Court Theatre. These were highly individual writers and they didn't want to be lumped together. But they did share a distrust of authority and an antipathy to upper-class clubbiness. Raised by lower-middle-class families (Amis, Wain, Osborne) or in working-class homes (Sillitoe, David Storey, Arnold Wesker) in provincial towns or cities, they were educated at grammar schools before some of them had government grants to the universities. Some came from the north of England. Yet they weren't

social critics: that role didn't interest them. Attuned to every-day
speech, they were impatient with literary Romanticism and with
those who worshiped "art." They thought poetry should be ac-
cessible, in no way mystifying. "Poetic" prose was contemptible.
Armed with irony, they lampooned the Establishment, the heritage of the public schools, and (at the start) were democratic. The
conversational, vernacular style of Amis's and Larkin's prose and
poetry was developed in letters between them, evident when
Amis later listed works and attitudes that exasperated him: "You
know, art novel, Pickarso, European thought, bourgeois conscience, Tuscany, Beckett, we haven't got a television set, lesson
of the master and nothing happening."

J. D Scott, literary editor of *The Spectator*, wrote that the new
writers were "anti-phoney, anti-wet; sceptical, robust, . . . prepared to be as comfortable as possible in a wicked, commercial"
world. Their appetite for American culture didn't extend to the
beats: Kerouac's "holiness" repelled them. Most loathed foreign
travel, which Bloomsbury had adored; they thought being
Abroad severed a writer from his roots and hence from his material. (Larkin said, "I wouldn't mind seeing China if I could come
back the same day.") Their fierce attention was trained on
England and the national values they impugned and satirized.
For them eloquence was fuel: their metaphors and their invective seemed to energize them as much as their convictions.
Language was a feast and a weapon, almost an end in itself.

Karl Miller, the *New Statesman*'s literary editor in the Sixties,
wrote that—to begin with—Amis and Larkin were seen as
"teddy-boy profaners of literature"; their writing snorted at
"good taste." Upstarts and outlaws were the antiheroes who liked
beer and sex and razzed the intelligentsia as much as the monar-
chists. Even Victor Gollancz, Amis's publisher, thought his *Lucky
Jim* was "vulgar." Leavis said Amis was a pornographer. But critics who abhorred these writers didn't seem to realize that much
of their work was meant to be funny. Amis called his novels

"serio-comedies." Osborne wanted *Look Back in Anger* to rouse "persistent laughter": the explosive Jimmy Porter's "'tirades' should be [performed] as arias"; the mutineer was "a one-man band, addressing himself to a world of shadows." Because I lived around the corner from the Royal Court, which I attended as if it were a neighborhood movie theater, I went to the play on its second night, four days before the electrifying Sunday reviews. (Tickets were cheap then, even for an austere budget like mine.) The *Times* review had been starchily contemptuous, so I was astounded by the wit and the vivacity, the gleeful insults springing from the young actors' lips, in fact I was thrilled.

At that time, theater was crucial to my life, as it was for many in London, which was witnessing a theatrical renaissance. Today's audiences, attuned to movies, may find it hard to imagine the magnetism of live acting. Greedy spectators not only went to the theater in droves, they talked about plays at length, they argued, they discussed interpretations and performances: the city was like a nonstop drama festival. Superb acting—from Laurence Olivier in *Titus Andronicus* and Michael Redgrave in Giraudoux's *Tiger at the Gates* to Alec Guinness and Irene Worth in Feydeau's hilarious *Hotel Paradiso*—could be taken for granted, and much of the public was ready for a new and thoroughly English theater.

Years afterward the London critic Irving Wardle observed that Osborne "really lived up to the Shakespearean maxim, 'Speak what we feel, not what we ought to say.'" His first play throbbed with jocular hatred, sexual sport, and a little love. "Blistering honesty," as Osborne called it, seemed to scorch the set during *Look Back in Anger*. Jimmy Porter charges that his high-toned mother-in-law is "as rough as a night in a Bombay brothel, and as tough as a matelot's arm" ("arse" before the censors read it), and says she ought to be dead: "My God, those worms will need a good dose of salts the day they get through with her! . . . She will pass away, my friends, leaving a trail of worms gasping for laxatives behind her—from purgatives to purgatory." Longing for his wife to suffer, he builds to a crescendo: "I want to stand up in your tears, and splash about in them, and sing. I want to be there when you grovel. . . . I want to watch it, I want the front seat. I want to see your face rubbed in the mud." His caustic contempt for postwar mentalities accelerates: "There aren't any good, brave causes left. If the big bang does come, and we all get killed off, it won't be in aid of the old-fashioned, grand design. It'll be just for the Brave New-nothing-very-much-thank you. About as pointless and inglorious as stepping in front of a bus." Toward the end he grows reflective: "Was I really wrong to believe that there's a—a kind of—burning virility of mind and spirit that looks for something as powerful as itself. . . . The voice that cries out doesn't *have* to be a weakling's, does it?" The leftover stoicism and stiff-upper-lipping of wartime Britain appeared to dissolve on the spot.

The play was advertised as "the English *Rebel Without a Cause*," and the traditional critics harped on Porter's lower-middle-class background, as though that were the source of his fury. But I felt I knew him: he was very like a schoolmate of mine, a wealthy young man from Connecticut, a privileged tornado. Osborne wrote that the character was initially viewed as "an unlikely freak" and later as "an archetype." I thought you could find him in any environment, income bracket, era, or country. Still, Osborne's contemporaries eagerly claimed him as a spokesman for their generation.

As Porter sneered and shouted week after week, the play set off great waves of excitement in the London theater, inciting experiments entirely new to the English stage. It was often said that Osborne revolutionized British theater. *Look Back in Anger* also stimulated managements to produce contemporary plays, as they hadn't before. Genteel drawing-room plays died almost at once; dramas of passion replaced them. The protagonists were usually poor and often witty. Osborne aimed to give his fellow citizens "lessons in feeling" while his work continued to be "full of private fires" (as he wrote about Tennessee Williams). Jimmy Porter's descendents may be the furious young Scotsmen of *Trainspotting*; steeped in poverty and heroin, they flaunt their "laddishness"—men behaving like teenage boys—in the comic tradition that Osborne pioneered. The lads of the 1990s didn't receive the education provided by the welfare state of the 1950s, but their wits seemed as sharp as their forebears'.

Praising the language of "a sophisticate, articulate lower class," Kenneth Tynan wrote that *Look Back in Anger* had "lanced a boil." Two years afterward Tynan observed that the play was "still reverberating," that "the new intelligentsia created by free education and state scholarships [had made] sizeable dents in the facade of public school culture." Upper-middle-class audiences and Oxbridge graduates applauded playwrights who attacked the values the elite had been raised with.

Osborne's young admirers were among those who were enraged by the Suez invasion, who flocked to the antinuclear demonstrations in Trafalgar Square and the Aldermaston marches on Easter weekends. The marchers grew younger year by year. Many of them, it appeared, were not political per se; they inhaled the anger in the air and directed it against the actions of the Tory government. When they voted for Labour they were making a gesture against the Establishment rather than aligning themselves with a program or a party. And if they had listened (very) closely, they would have heard that Osborne's leading males were railing against the welfare state and the lower middle classes, not the upper. In the Seventies, Osborne, Amis, Larkin, and Braine emerged as extreme right-wingers; by then it was acknowledged that they hadn't been subversives or even progressives. But the atmosphere they'd created had generated some vital and sinewy British films that explored working-class sensibilities, starting with *Room at the Top*: its success generated a market and an audience for *Saturday Night and Sunday Morning, Billy*

*Liar, The Loneliness of the Long Distance Runner,* and *This Sporting Life.*

Still other currents were racing through the London theater. The ebullience of Brendan Behan's uproarious *Hostage* and seventeen-year-old Shelagh Delaney's *Taste of Honey* were developed out of Joan Littlewood's Theatre Workshop in the East End, where improvisation abounded and radical politics outdistanced the liberal-left skepticism of the Royal Court. Littlewood's cheerful ambition was to destroy middle-class theater. (Still, her enthusiastic audiences were mainly middle-class.) And the widespread disdain for organized religion may have enabled the first production in English of Samuel Beckett's *Waiting for Godot* to become a cultural milestone. (I remember the exultant audience during the intermission on the first night, but few of us would have foreseen a long run for the play or its perpetual revivals.) Clearly *Waiting for Godot* also moved people who were afflicted with spiritual hungers. And despite the general aversion to metaphysics, Beckett's shambling derelicts and depressives, fugitives from silent-comedy two-reelers, enthralled spectators who were cool to the Christianity in Eliot's plays and Graham Greene's *Potting Shed.* In the latter a priest strikes a bargain with God, relinquishing his faith so that a dead nephew may be brought back to life. Greene's stature as a novelist was almost ignored while critics hooted at that play.

In the meantime the fathers of the Theatre of the Absurd—Ionesco and Genet as well as Beckett—were welcomed in the context of comedy. (Harold Pinter's first plays weren't much appreciated—Tynan called *The Birthday Party* "a clever fragment grown dropsical with symbolic content"—but Pinter soon commanded an audience to rival Beckett's.) The idea that life is ludicrous, especially because it can be so easily lost, suited Britain in the atomic age. Tynan predicted that "satire, irony, gallows humor and other mutations of the comic spirit" would thrive in the English theater, whereas "tragedy, with its traditional respect for hierarchies and its passion for bloody denouements, has little to say to a rebellious generation obsessed by the danger of imminent megadeaths." Amid the lunacies of the nuclear arms race, Tynan argued that the most serious writers were also humorous, and he chided some Absurdists for their "tone of privileged despair."

In 1956 Bertolt Brecht's Berliner Ensemble visited London; watching *The Caucasian Chalk Circle* I could see that six months' rehearsal meant that every footstep, each half-smile, was significant and stunning. I was fascinated by the stylized miming of the corrupt masked aristocrats and the bare-faced, thigh-slapping earthiness of the peasants, who weren't noble: some were likable, some were brutes. As a young woman strode rhythmically around a revolving stage, a baby strapped to her back and a stout wooden staff in her hand, you sensed the harshness of her long journey over a mountain and across a glacier—yet her plain lumpy face suddenly became beautiful when she smiled. An illogically happy ending sent one out of the theater feeling elated, though I was still too apolitical to grasp the range of Brecht's Marxism.

Tynan remarked that Brecht's plays revealed "a passionate desire to improve the human condition." While that was hardly Osborne's concern, *The Entertainer* bristled with Brechtian details, such as the sarcastic songs beamed at the audience while Laurence Olivier—the failing music-hall comedian who admits he's "dead behind the eyes," incapable of emotion—cackles and shudders his way through images of self-destruction, which the playwright felt were uniquely English. Osborne had said he'd been "blessed" with one of "God's greatest gifts: to be born English." Probably his cohorts felt much the same: far from being nationalists or even patriots, they could be glad that their country gave them subjects that stimulated their indignation, provided them with targets for ridicule, and made their language soar.

Before I came to England I'd had the notion that the British were reserved, indeed repressed. So I was unprepared for the scatter-shot frankness I encountered as soon as I arrived in London. At a grand dinner party in Belgravia I listened to a suave young man, a recent Cambridge luminary, prattling about alcoholic actors: "Now take Robert Newton—"

Hostess (brightly, no malice): "Oh! He's my brother. Did you see him act while he was drunk?"

Young Man: "No! no! I meant I once saw him play the *role* of a drunken man, I don't mean he was drunk, but he was acting the part of someone who—"

Hostess: "Yes, I saw that. He was drunk."

At formal dinners I was often seated next to strangers who promptly told me details of their sexual experiences at their public schools—one said Eton had ruined his life. And where would he send his son? "Why, Eton." A woman fondly quoted her uncle, who was asked by a clerk in a men's boutique, "What is your pleasure, sir?" and replied, "My pleasure is fucking, but what I really want is a white tie." Another male dinner partner told me after some fifteen minutes' acquaintance that he'd been seduced at eleven by his brother-in-law: that had upset his sister.

Rapidly I found that sexual candor was matched by dramatic indiscretions: everybody seemed to inform everybody about their own and others' most intimate moments. (I was sure that everything that happened in London also occurred in New York, but the English *talked* about it so much.) Some tales may have been apocryphal, but perhaps not: the Duchess of Windsor was said to have perfected "the Cleopatra clutch," contracting her vaginal muscles more forcefully than most women did. One heard that Kenneth Tynan liked spanking, collected whips, and that he joked about it: "Just a thong at twilight." (He was also charmed by what he called "the riddle of the sphincter.") There was an elderly cabinet minister whose favorite pastime was playing horse: being harnessed to a small carriage and then trotting around his large garden. One day when he answered the phone and the caller complained that he couldn't understand him, the minister said, "Juft a moment, muft take the bit out of my mouf." And I was told that the late Duff Cooper, once ambassador to France, had been "such a nice man, but he *would* keep fucking his nieces." I also heard that London, no longer Paris, was the center of the sex industry, a bazaar where newfangled golden showers and houses catering to special tastes—prostitutes dressed as nuns and clients who became Hitler or Mussolini—were even more profitable than on the Continent. When the Profumo case—which revealed that a politician had far-flung excursions among call girls—seized the headlines in 1963, it startled Americans at home but not those who'd lived in London.

In Manhattan I'd been accustomed to the random polygamy of my parents' world of writers; apart from serious affairs that often led to divorce and remarriage, unexpected encounters (mainly after a lot of drinks) were frequent. Jealousy was frowned on: those who came of age in the Twenties considered themselves free spirits, and they felt that husbands and wives shouldn't be treated as possessions. Of course many were hurt and angry when their spouses roamed. But they tried not to let those feelings show: pride and dignity were at stake. In London, however, much of the coupling and reshuffling of my seniors seemed deliberate. Playing games and winning them appeared essential to sexual life. There was ongoing intrigue, as though some could not bear to have a lasting relationship. "Infidelity"—a word I've always disliked—seemed to be carefully calculated among those who resisted being tied down: the wanderers wanted their partners to know that they weren't the only dolphins in the sea. It was said that Cyril Connolly usually wished to shed his latest conquest as soon as it was achieved. Still, there was remorse when he wrote, "As we leave others, so shall we be left." Within a circle of overlapping liaisons, the costume designer Jocelyn Rickards wrote that she smeared her lipstick on A. J. Ayer's pillow, where the philosopher's one-night stands would see it. (Ayer was sometimes called "the open-fly man of London." John Osborne observed, "As a sought-after cocksman, Ayer had one unenviable advantage: a cold heart." In Ayer's view, philosophy was "an abstract activity" that had nothing to do with life.) There were others who appeared to feast on jealousy as though it were an addictive stimulant. So you heard a lively amount of sexual boasting, as if that made the swaggerer desirable. What you didn't hear much about was love—unlike sex, it seemed to be an embarrassing subject.

I was told that the sexual sprees were partly a habit acquired in wartime, when young people going off to the front or dwelling through the Blitz felt that only a few weeks (or maybe days) might be left to them. If death was on the doorstep, you could at least enjoy tonight. The silent V-2 rockets, each weighing fourteen tons and traveling without sound, exploded violently when they landed without warning—roaring and blazing just before one's death. And if life was to end so suddenly, why spend it with one person? Elizabeth Bowen wrote that it was a time of "unmarriedness." In the highly charged atmosphere of war-torn London, living precariously appeared to enlarge sexual appetites and intensify the emotions: spontaneous sex could seem even more erotic than in peacetime. I was also told that having several lovers at once could make someone feel less likely to be killed by a bomb or a bullet—a species of magical thinking.

My own present-day situation was changeable. In the year and a half before I met my future husband, I played with a young American and two Englishmen. The American, a good-humored editor with a galloping sexual appetite, rather disapproved of women willing to hit the hay with him, and kept saying that Brits were randier than our compatriots. He thought he should confine himself to hookers but didn't manage to. One of the

Englishmen was a photographer whose merry cynicism was quickened by the ad agencies; given a rigid chunk of cheese with the slogan "Spreads Like Butter," finding it impossible to cut, he asked for a pound of butter and photographed that. He took a grim glee in the evidence that many pictures made food look repulsive. My other Englishman was a pensive baritone who sang (as I did) with the London Bach Group and practiced corporate law. He said he enjoyed risk; he took flying lessons and climbed icy mountains.

I liked Englishmen, liked their decisiveness, their quick, rude, charming speech, and I liked uncircumcised men, but I didn't fall for anyone. I was discovering that sex could be delectable without love—not what a romantic wanted to know. I missed the great surges and swells of emotion. The Pill was available in England before it was at home; delighted to ditch my diaphragm, I kept hoping that love would catch me by surprise, though I didn't think you could precipitate it. Reading Colette, I was touched when she remarked, "And what of the monogamous blood that ran in my veins so inconveniently?" I felt like a closet monogamist, but there was no reason to live that way. Those encounters put me on good terms with my body, made me more tolerant of its imperfections: legs too long for a short torso, a vague waistline, breasts larger than I wanted. Meanwhile I dodged clumsy passes from unattractive men who seemed predatory because most women didn't want them. Some were potential employers; I rebelled at the pressures to trade sex for work, and the refusals cost me a couple of assignments. In those days the concept of sexual harassment on the job did not exist.

In 1956 Walker Evans was in England on a series of assignments for *Fortune*. The editor Sonia Orwell was arranging a reception for him and Jean Stafford; Evans invited me and then advised me not to go. Why not? Because when he'd mentioned me to his hostess, she said, "Just what I need for Cyril." (Connolly's second wife had left him for the second time and he was briefly between diversions.) Evans explained that Sonia, the widow of George Orwell, was "a literary moll" who "pimped"— he corrected himself—"found girlfriends" for her favorite writers and loved to interfere with others' lives. Evans told me I would be in way over my head if I met Connolly and then dined with him even once: if I didn't sleep with him, he would be vengeful and would do me tremendous harm professionally, telling editors not to publish or hire me. That would be the end of writing for the *New Statesman* or anywhere else. In short, he could be downright vicious, indeed dangerous when his pride was hurt.

From John Davenport I already knew the scope of Connolly's power and I was determined to avoid him. I was also repelled by accounts of office life at *Horizon*, his great magazine of the Forties, where a batch of melancholy young female acolytes were browbeaten by the master, humbly fulfilling his every requirement as he brandished a psychic whip. *Horizon* was even called an S and M scene, editorially speaking. It sounded as though he was terribly dependent on women but didn't much like them. I understood that the magazine had been vital to British culture during the war, that it had helped to keep the arts alive when civilization itself seemed imperiled. But I was glad that I hadn't crossed its threshold.

By then I was also entranced with Connolly's celebration of the physical world—the peaches and pineapples and lobsters, lemurs and Mediterranean seascapes, radiant sunlight and lyrical sex—and I was moved by what Evelyn Waugh called "the authentic waste-land despair." I thought (and I still do) that Connolly wrote some of the finest prose of the century. The excitement of reading *The Unquiet Grave* for the first time returns whenever I look through it for an image: the winged vocabulary, the passion for language, the supple use of myths seem as fresh today as when the sentences were new to me. But I recoiled from several of the themes of his "word cycle": that the goal of a love affair was to be cured of love and that first love was by far the best, that later ones were inevitably disappointing. And with masochistic gusto he made himself dislikable. So this fat man wasn't going to be my friend. But at the last moment Evans persuaded me to go to the reception: he said it would be "high cheese," redolent of Bloomsbury, and he would protect me from Connolly.

At the door of a cramped and crowded Percy Street flat in Soho, Sonia Orwell—blond, flushed, and puffy in a bunched-up salmon-colored dress—clutched me: "Here's my little American!" She hauled me toward a baggy shape in a corner, but Evans caught my arm and led me away from it. In the small stuffy living room, hot for an English summer, I saw Dwight Macdonald, newly settled in London for a year of editing at *Encounter*, Ruth Ford and her husband Zachary Scott, who would soon open in a stage version of Faulkner's *Requiem for a Nun* at the Royal Court, and a squinting, semi-scowling man who hopped from one foot to the other as he talked: Lucian Freud. Momentarily the crowd parted and a small figure stood holding out a glass of wine toward me: "I am Clive Bell," he said, then disappeared as bodies surrounded him. John Lehmann, editor of *London Magazine*, and his sister, the novelist Rosamond Lehmann—a graceful silvery-white galleon in full sail—spoke cordially to me, but my mouth was too dry for talking. Breathless and bossy, Sonia Orwell grabbed me again and dragged me over to Connolly, who squashed me against the wall. He had light blue eyes and the smooth blubbery lips of a baby. I was angry as well as unnerved. He said something about having once been "marooned in Baltimore" and I croaked, "How?" He pretended to be an American Indian, raising his right hand, grunting "Ugh! How!" and shaking his pink jowls. Evans quickly rescued me again and I felt I'd escaped from a bloodsucker, an arch-parasite who could drain the young of vitality.

E. M. Forster had said that Connolly gave pleasure a bad

name, and the Orwell party reminded me of Forster's image of
"odors from the abyss": an ominous scent of disasters to come.

Soon thereafter I went off to Andalusia for several weeks;
there the light green waves breaking on the shores of Algeciras
washed away the London angst. The salt air was fresh, the water
so clear that you could see veins of red clay in the sand. Three
small boys joined me in exploring a rock pool where we found a
live starfish as big as my head. Floating on my back in that bay
ringed with mountains, staring past my big toe at the Rock of
Gibraltar, I felt safe from the Orwellian flesh-eaters who would
consume one's heart and liver if they had a chance.

More than three months later I was chatting uneasily with John
Raymond—not yet crocked—at a party in Egerton Crescent,
when I saw a white-haired stranger with a rather handsome oval
face watching me through gimlet eyes. He walked toward us and
purposefully tossed a large glass of red wine all over the seat of
Raymond's trousers. "Oh my dear fellow, I'm frightfully sorry."
"Will it stain? Will it stain?" The man apologized, advised
Raymond to pour cold water on his pants, handed him a five-
pound note for the cleaning bill, and smoothly introduced
himself to me: Alexander Haverford. As Raymond stumbled
miserably away, Haverford said he was sorry he'd "had to do
that," but there was no other way to dispose of Raymond and he
had to speak to me. I remembered that he was an editor at the
dying *Picture Post* and was known as "the most romantic man in
London" because he always got married: his life was a sequence
of divorces and new nuptials with scarcely a lull in between.
Why had he soaked John Raymond? Because he and Constance
wanted me to come to dinner a fortnight hence. I hardly knew
Constance—a vivid post-deb in her mid-twenties with a piercing
voice who came on like a junior Sonia Orwell—and I'd kept my

distance because she seemed manipulative. Now she was
Haverford's latest bride-to-be. I said I was tied up on the date he
mentioned, so he changed it. Seeing no way out, I accepted the
puzzling invitation.

That fall I was living in West Kensington, quite a way through
a thick November fog to Haverford's home in Pimlico. The gush
of welcome from my barely known hosts made the occasion all
the more perplexing. I'd expected other guests, but the table was
laid for four. We had little to say to one another. Then Connolly
walked in. So I realized that the whole evening was a set-up.

I didn't leap to my feet and spit on the floor or smash an antique vase or shout horrible curses at them, but I wished I could
vanish in a sandstorm. Connolly said it was nice to see me again.
Conversation was hardly necessary because he was a soloist, a vir-
tuoso performer who held the center of the stage. Throughout
dinner he told stories and I listened only fitfully as he parodied
the Queen's recent broadcast—he was a splendid mimic—and
talked about a woman who was "so frightfully fond of fucking"
that she'd forbidden him to smoke when they were in her weekend cottage; she thought nicotine deadened the libido. We had
veal nicely flavored with lemon but hard to chew. (Surely it took
courage to cook for Connolly—of a birthday dinner for Ezra
Pound he wrote, "I shall never forget the white truffles in cheese
sauce and it took them a long time to forget me.") Deadpan I
mentioned an essay by John Davenport and Connolly spoke most
respectfully of him; after Davenport's devastating review of
Connolly's novel-in-progress, I had to appreciate that flash of
decency.

Over dessert (crème brûlée) Connolly said he had a problem.
Brightly our hosts asked what it was. Well, several articles of his
had been translated for a French publication—which could pay
him only in francs. So he had to use the cash in Paris. But that
glorious city could be dispiriting for a solitary traveler: he needed
a companion. Constance and Haverford seemed suddenly in-

spired: how about Nora? What a good idea, he said—and then
offered them a portion of the money: he would spend the equivalent of sixty pounds on me and give them "a nice present" if
I went with him. As they gaily urged me to go, I said nothing,
smiling faintly, frozen in my silence. Connolly said, "Perhaps the
little lady needs to think it over," as though I weren't there.

The crème brûlée was too rich for three of us to finish it, but
Connolly nipped around the table and spooned up what we'd
left; soon the sticky stuff was smeared all over his cheeks, but he
didn't wipe it off as he licked his spoon. Constance put on a new
record—"See You Later, Alligator"—and he began to dance to it
by himself, waving his traveler's checks and chanting, "Money!
Money! Money! Money! Who'll take my checks! Who'll come to
Paris . . ." As he bounced up and down, I noticed that his jowls
had lost their summer pinkness and were now yellow, that his
belly billowed. Constance led me to the bedroom; she was furious: they needed money—*Picture Post* would soon fold—and besides, Connolly could do marvelous things for my career. I shook
my head, and her vexation mounted as we rejoined the men.

More elaborate stories while I calculated how to get away on
my own. There was a lengthy fuss over a liqueur—something
rare and special—and when Connolly accepted a second glass,
that seemed the ideal moment for departure: surely he wouldn't
leave his drink unfinished. As I said good-bye, he flung his head
back and emptied his glass, announcing that we would share a
taxi.

A long ride ahead: the fog had intensified and was coiling in
faster. He had hardly spoken to me directly, but in the cab he put
his arm around my shoulders and said he'd forgotten my last
name. I foresaw exactly what would happen: he would be insulted when I pulled back from his fondlings and angered when I
turned down the Paris trip as politely as possible. Then my writing and working life in London would be over and I'd have to
return to my parents' home in New York. I wished that lightning

would strike the taxi, that Connolly would have a cerebral hemorrhage, that the driver would go mad. The arm tightened as Connolly bundled closer to me on the seat, asking what Sayre meant; he said he loved to know the origin of names. Glumly I said, "Sooth-sayer." He squeezed me, he was excited: "You must tell my fortune!" I said I didn't know how.

I lost another ten inches of the seat as his bulk seemed to swell: soon it would fill the entire cab. Squeeze, squeeze—he said he *must* hear his fortune: would it be "nice or nasty? Nice or nasty?" To my astonishment I found myself saying "Nasty." He flinched in distress: "But why?" I told him it depended on whether he liked being restless or not. "*Restless!* Oh I hate it, I'm a peace-seeker." He said he longed for stability and calm. As though from far away I heard my voice informing him that his future would be restless. The arm was withdrawn. In an anguished tone he said, "Restless—because alone?" Then I knew just what I was doing: "Yes, because you'll be alone."

He retreated to the opposite side of the seat and murmured that being alone was what he dreaded most, it was the worst punishment he knew. The ogre was gone: beside me there was just a fat man with empty eyes. We rode in silence for a while. I felt fine. Then he asked if I was soon leaving London. I said I was staying on. Abruptly he rapped on the glass behind the driver, told him to stop, paid him, wished me luck—luck!—and hastened away in the fog, almost scampering across the pavement, something threatening left behind. Certain that he would do me no damage from now on, I marveled at my magical escape. I also felt rather like a sibyl: until the very end I hadn't known what I was going to say—it had been like an out-of-body experience. So I stretched out my legs in the taxi and enjoyed the slow ride home. As the fog wrapped around the cab I promised myself to make notes.

Some months afterward I was at the theater with a jovial barrister; we were seeing Racine's *Phèdre* with Edwige Feuillère. At the intermission Connolly lurched up to him, not looking at me: "That's a terrible girl you're with!" My escort, who was fond of him, laughed and asked what was the matter. "She told me a bad fortune—and it's all come true!" Connolly scuttled off and my friend asked what on earth that was about. After I told him the whole story, his laughter rose again and he said that was what often happened to bullies: their demands rebounded like boomerangs. Bullies, he added, were usually cowards—who feared that their bullying wouldn't be successful. In effect, Connolly had told his own fortune. Still, I was happy to take the credit.

# IV.

Streaked with dried red clay from the beaches of Algeciras, where I'd been swimming only a few hours before I flew back to London, I ran down the long hallway of Flat Seven, 32 Kensington Court. I thought the apartment was empty—Mai Zetterling was out—and I longed for a hot bath. Rushing into the bathroom I nearly collided with a tall man in a tailored suit, his dark head bent over the tub, water bursting noisily from the faucet. He said, "You must be Nora" and introduced himself, but I didn't hear his name as the tap screeched over the roaring bathwater. He explained that there was a plumbing crisis in his nearby home and that Mai had offered her bathroom. But—noticing my streaky arms—he suggested that I take the first bath. And would I run his when I was done? He looked a bit familiar but I couldn't place him.

I was between lodgings and Mai had invited me to stay on my return from Spain. That evening two documentary film-makers from Copenhagen were on hand and the kitchen was humming: Mai was stuffing avocados with prawns—one of her favorite dishes)—the Danes were beating eggs and whipping up some kind of sauce; I was making a tomato salad (as I often would in

Flat Seven); and the handsome man from the bathroom was de-
canting wine, so there was no chance to ask about him. At dinner
all the talk was about theater, about live performances, especially
the Berliner Ensemble's *Mother Courage,* and I almost asked the
courtly stranger if he had connections with the stage. But instinct
warned me not to.

On the brink of dessert, Mai's children dashed into the living
room, which was furnished in cool pale grays and whites, Scandinavian teak—while the children seemed to belong in a hot cli-
mate. Swarthy and shaggy, young for their age and voluble, they
were excited by seeing guests. Etienne, who was eleven, had been
baking all afternoon, a frenzy of anxious production. Louis, age
nine, whooped when he saw the icing on one of her small cakes:
it said "Try One." "It's not *try* one, silly," he cried, "It's Tyrone!"
Then I knew who had run my bath.

Mai and the Danish couple had called him "Trrone," with a
little Scandinavian trill on the *r,* so I hadn't caught on before.
While I'd been in Spain, Mai had been acting in a new movie:
*Abandon Ship!,* a lifeboat drama in which the leading man was
Tyrone Power. Together they had spent many sopping hours in a
chilly water tank surrounded by wind machines at Shepperton
Studios. I'd seen only one of Power's forty movies (a revival of
*Alexander's Ragtime Band* when I was in my teens), so I hadn't rec-
ognized him. Most of his postwar films had been costume sagas
—*Prince of Foxes* and *The Black Rose*—or sluggish romances, and
although I wasn't a movie snob those pictures hadn't tempted me.

That evening I was impressed by how much he knew about
the theater—and by his unassuming manner. A radiant sexuality
had made him one of Twentieth Century–Fox's brightest con-
stellations in the mid-Thirties and into the Forties—at one point,
only MGM's Mickey Rooney was ahead of him at the box office,
by a slim margin—and huge crowds of fans had mobbed him
wherever he went. In 1942 he was ranked as Hollywood's most
popular male star. I would soon learn that in his early twenties

he'd signed an inflexible contract which committed him to many
feeble movies, that as the years passed Twentieth Century Fox
and producer Darryl Zanuck had treated him like a witless com-
modity, almost a piece of meat, although he had been Zanuck's
protégé since 1936. Power would have understood today's Hollywood, where actors can become merchandise, all too easily. His
career had sagged badly after the war. (His only successful movie
of that period was the ponderous *Razor's Edge.*) Recently he'd
formed his own independent company, Copa Productions, planning to make just a few films and to concentrate on the stage,
which meant far more to him than motion pictures. At forty-two
he was resolved on renewal, indeed hoping to change his entire
life, mainly by finding strong roles and directors, escaping
Hollywood as much as possible, and allying himself with people
he truly respected.

After dinner he suddenly clapped a hand over one eye: a
cinder. As Mai leaned over him, delicately lifting his lid with
her thumb and telling him to blink, I realized that they were a
couple and that she was in love with him.

But I'm getting ahead of my story. I'd admired Mai's acting
since my school days, when the Swedish *Torment* (also known as
*Frenzy*, directed by Alf Sjöberg) and the British *Frieda* were
shown in New York. In the former, shot when Mai was nineteen,
she was a tattered shop girl who dies toward the end of the film:
was she stricken with heart failure or was she murdered? Ingmar
Bergman, who co-wrote the script—it was his first screen credit—never told her. She was amused by the mystery and *Torment*
made her an international star. *Frieda,* directed by Basil Dearden,
centered on the cruelties inflicted on a German bride of an RAF
officer in a small English country town. Anti-German feeling
was still so fierce in the late Forties that British film producers
didn't dare to hire a German actress but sought out a Swede.

Born in a town famous for its gherkins, the illegitimate daughter of a working-class woman, Mai didn't meet her father—an

affluent middle-class businessman—until she was thirty-one.
She began acting in a children's theater club when she was about
fourteen, then had a scholarship to the National Theater School
of Stockholm. Before she was twenty she had major classical roles
in the Royal Dramatic Theater, appearing in *Twelfth Night,*
Lorca's *House of Bernarda Alba,* and Chekhov's *Three Sisters.*
Sartre called her "an important tragedienne of the century" when
she played his Electra in *The Flies* at twenty-three.

Settled in England after *Frieda*, under contract to J. Arthur
Rank, she kept being cast as a forlorn refugee in a kerchief and
belted raincoat, wandering through the rubble of bombed cities.
Occasionally she was a purring femme fatale, directed to widen
her eyes under archly raised brows while she slowly pulled off
her long black gloves. At that time the Rank organization had
signed many highly talented performers but didn't provide good
scripts for them: the studio's main product was an avalanche of
third-rate movies with distinguished stars. But Mai won abundant praise on the London stage as Hedwig in Ibsen's *Wild Duck*
and Nora in his *Doll's House,* Nina in Chekhov's *Sea Gull,* and
Euridice in Jean Anouilh's *Point of Departure.*

Some years after that, I met her in the context of the Cold War:
a young American writer, whose blacklisted family had moved
to London, was living with Mai in the mid-Fifties. He was a
friend of my American boyfriend at Oxford, and the four of us
used to go to the theater or on picnics together. But because I'd
been away during Mai's weeks in the Shepperton tank, I didn't
know how radically her life had altered—until she coaxed a cinder from Tyrone Power's eye.

When you entered Flat Seven, pushing past a heavy orange wool
curtain with white stripes that hung over the front door, you were
in a very private kingdom: Mai shunned the world outside. As it

happened I stayed in the apartment for ten months; it was large enough to sustain everyone's privacy, sheltered in a Victorian brick building in a byway off Kensington High Street: the place wasn't easy to find. Today, thinking of Mai throughout several decades—in London, New York, Stockholm, and the South of France—reminds me that she developed in different directions after her Kensington years. But she maintained her allegiance to Mozart and van Gogh, her love of gardening, cats, truffles, honeycomb on toast and duck with oranges, and her hatred of cities. She liked writers; although she didn't have an ear for English prose or poetry, she valued those who did.

Small and slender, blond, with a long nose and a wide mouth in a mobile face, she could seem both fragile and rugged, refined or bawdy. She saw herself as vulnerable yet was aware of her own strength: her will was probably the most powerful I've known. Determination—to perform in plays of her choice (and later to write and direct)—enabled her to raise whirlwinds. An adventurer who relished risks, she had no regard for obstacles. Told that a specific task was impossible, she was almost sure to achieve it: transforming an old house or getting a play produced or finding money from nowhere for a film. As she often said, she loved organizing: assembling a cast to act with her in Anouilh's *Sauvage,* arranging expeditions—to the woods in early spring to gather forsythia, to the sea, to Lapland, to Sicily—or preparing a colossal feast of gourmet foods from Harrods when she could hardly pay the phone bill. As her overdraft grew, her meals became more costly: caviar gleamed in the fridge and at Sunday dinners her daughter innocently groaned, "Oh God, strawberries *again.*"

Mai was gifted at galvanizing others, at exhorting them to accomplish what they wanted. "You *must* do it," she used to say to those who were hesitating over a new project or were unconfident about it. In her early thirties she was also quite gleeful about what experience had taught her: she kept telling me that *"years* make the difference," that you couldn't skip any chapters of your life or understand certain things until you'd lived longer. This was brave for an actress, whose profession deplored the passage of time. But it was a sign of rebellion too: she would not pretend to stop growing.

Mai despised Hollywood because of the one movie she'd made there—playing a testy psychiatrist in *Knock on Wood* with Danny Kaye—but I had a soft spot for it. I'd gone to nursery school and kindergarten in Beverly Hills while my father wrote *Annie Oakley,* the final script of *Gunga Din,* and parts of other movies, and I'd revisited as a teenager. I liked Hollywood lore: the tales told by screenwriters Nunnally Johnson, Frances Goodrich and Albert Hackett, and my father. But most references to the American film industry raised shudders in Kensington Court. Still, Power didn't like snobbery about Hollywood, despite his many bad experiences there, and he admired what Orson Welles and Charles Laughton had accomplished in the movie business. And some of Power's recollections were more humorous than Mai's. He recalled that he used to deal with the Hays Office by sitting next to the censor during an advance screening—and asking for a light or offering one just when a racy scene began. But what if the censor didn't smoke? Power said he'd dropped a pen or a pair of sunglasses on the floor at the right moments or even spilled a little coffee on the man's sleeve.

Mai laughed at that story, but she recoiled from manipulation. She described sitting with Danny Kaye by his Hollywood pool when he'd bullied his other guests into swimming naked so that he could see "how things changed shape in the water." She didn't laugh when Power returned from drinks at Kenneth Tynan's Mayfair apartment, where the host had cajoled his theatrical guests into joining a game: he would give a pound to anyone who could cry within one minute. Power refused, but the rest flooded at once and Tynan walked around handing out pound notes. (While I had great respect for Tynan's criticism and his prose,

I didn't take to him on occasional meetings: he seemed patronizing, even to his best friends, and so mannered that I unfairly
thought his stutter was fake, an attempt at chic.) Knowing that
many theater people were afraid of him, Mai didn't want to meet
him; even though Tynan had given her favorable reviews, she
suspected that he was malicious.

Wearing a bandanna and dark glasses or a fur hat pulled down
over her ears, Mai could escape notice in London. But Power was
still pestered in public; it was even worse, he said, than in American cities. Hence many of their evenings were spent in her home
or his. But Mai was very fond of a little Soho restaurant called
the Old Venezia, and they once arranged to dine in a private
room upstairs. With greedy anticipation they ordered the first
course—and then waited at length for food that never came.
Finally Mai went downstairs to complain. The manager was astonished to see her; as part of their antipasto they'd asked for
beetroot, and she learned that was a code: any couple who requested that dish was presumed to be having sex and mustn't be
interrupted. Power found that marvelously funny and said he
could hardly think of anything more uncomfortable than "fucking in a small restaurant."

Mai's talent for places was a boon to her friends: for one Easter
week she rented a Victorian houseboat anchored in a bay (locally
called a bag) off the coast of Devon, surrounded by hills covered
with gorse and primroses, where a group of us caught lobsters
and large crabs. Back in London I used to go riding in Hampstead; Mai decided to come too, vowing to learn, which she did.
As we cantered over the heath, she planned a horseback trip in
Crete: she and Power, the children and I, we must do that *soon*.
We never did, but Mai's impulsive nature made each scheme
seem concrete: she could cause you to believe that you were
halfway to the island of the Minotaur.

Facing a channel of the Baltic, one of Mai's most enchanted
domiciles would be a vast nineteenth-century wooden mansion

outside Stockholm, where she lived while directing a film in 1964. It had been built for the physician of King Oscar II; there were towers and carved staircases and silvery views of the water. The film studio furnished it with sets from Ingmar Bergman's movies: I slept in a bed used in *Through a Glass Darkly,* on sheets from *The Devil's Eye,* we ate at a long dining table from *The Seventh Seal,* and other furniture came from *Smiles of a Summer Night.* On first crossing the threshold I was astounded to see so much familiar decor—in a country where I'd never been before. The lampshades were made by the woman who'd designed Garbo's hats for one of her early Swedish silents. The shabby shades had such presence that one almost bowed in passing. No electricity: we lived by candle light among props, which pleased Mai as she tackled her first full-length movie.

I relished the company of actors and I think they liked mine because I wasn't one. I'd acted a bit in college and knew I wasn't good in serious roles, but I had enjoyed playing comic scenes. I loved the sound of an audience's laughter. Still, I had no wish to be an actress, preferring to write and aware that I didn't have what acting required: the ability to become a whole series of be-ings—a maniac, a princess, a thief, a ghost, a spy. Some major performers—Alec Guinness, Peggy Ashcroft, Ralph Richardson—seemed to lose their identities as they vanished into a role; others used different parts of their own characters or their experiences. Mai did both: she was a hateful Hedda Gabler—almost unrecognizable to a friend—and a hardy yet lyrical wayfarer much like herself.

Unlike most earthlings, she seemed nearly immune to surprise. When Graham Greene, an unexpected dinner guest in Kensington, peered around a door frame and asked with a mischievous boy's smile, "May I bring my Chinaman from Hong Kong?" she said "Of course" without missing a beat. With a swift nod, Greene summoned the man, who stood waiting in the hallway. (Reviewing movies in the Thirties, Greene had called

Charlie Chan "an astute Chinaman," and his usage hadn't changed in two decades.) Mai hardly knew Greene, but he was then involved with her good friend Anita Björk, the Swedish actress known for her stunning performance in the film of Strindberg's *Miss Julie*. I remember that the whites of Greene's blue eyes were rather bloodshot; even when he smiled he looked like someone who existed under pressure and with stress. He was affable throughout the seafood salads and platters of smoked fish, except for a moment when a young American man referred to "a state of grace," using the term metaphorically. Greene glared: "*Grace*? What do *you* mean by grace?" That sudden spurt of hostility was almost frightening, and the rest of us fell silent. Apparently those who dwelled outside the Church had no right to borrow its language—even though Greene was at odds with some of its doctrines. (As he aged, he said he had ceased to believe in sexual sin.)

Later he described himself to his friend V. S. Pritchett as "a Catholic atheist." Yet the Church still gripped him. Mai told me that when Anita visited him in London, he wished her to play the role of a hidden "mistress": he wanted her to wear large hats and veils and was reluctant to introduce her to his literary friends —even her presence in the city should be a secret from them. Mai said the spirited Anita could not conform to behavior that made him feel satisfyingly sinful; she couldn't share the sense of guilt he found exciting. Mai often exaggerated, but that story seemed to echo the themes of transgression in Greene's novels.

At Mai's dinner, asked his opinion of the movie of *The End of the Affair* with Deborah Kerr and Van Johnson, Greene laughed and made a dismissive gesture but said that the movie sale of *The Quiet American* had enabled him to buy a ranch in Canada for his daughter, who wanted to raise cattle. ("I can't think why, she's a rather pretty girl.") He said that soon after the purchase, oil was struck on the land—making it too valuable for cattle farming. In London he'd taken his daughter to see Irene Worth in Ugo Betti's

*The Queen and the Rebels,* which made her weep, "and I thought she seemed almost human." Years afterward I read that before she was born he'd called her "the amoeba," and that he and his wife had considered having her adopted.

Divorced from Tutte Lemkow, the Norwegian dancer and choreographer Mai had married at nineteen, with whom she had the two children, she remained on good terms with him. But she repeatedly declared that marriage meant mutual destruction, a slow death, that only neurotics wanted to get married. In her Kensington era, her genuine joie de vivre was flavored with a subtle pessimism: she frequently asserted that happiness was not a goal, that a quest for happiness could derail one's existence. Later she continued to denounce marriage during the rewarding years with her second husband.

One of her oldest friends remarked that she combined magic with passion, and the unexpected seemed to occur around or near her. Picnicking close to Bushey Heath with her children, she and I were intrigued by a very tall pair of eighteenth-century gates in front of a long alley lined with poplars; we saw a hideous semi-Victorian manor house in the distance. Mai said we *had* to explore that tantalizing vista. So we crawled through a hole in a wire fence and found a whole series of wild and formal gardens. No one in sight. We picked armloads of exotic blossoms and learned later that we'd plundered a great lord's estate; many of the rare flowers were from South America. Usually trespassers were heavily fined or even arrested, but we were never caught. Being protected from unforeseen events seemed natural in Mai's vicinity. She owned a gilded metal belt from India which hung low on the left hip; part of it dangled down one's thigh. I called it "the magic belt" and Mai insisted that I wear it on the evening I met Connolly (though I didn't know I was going to). Delighted by the outcome, she said the belt had saved me from disaster.

By the time I came to know Tyrone Power he was no longer a flawless beauty; his features had weathered, the deep-set eyes had sunk a little farther into his skull, the chin line was imperfect. But the smile was still like sunrise, and the gaiety he brought into a room was contagious. I thought he resembled a Scott Fitzgerald character: he appeared to have the "romantic readiness" of Gatsby along with the social grace and generosity of Dick Diver; he seemed eager to hear what others were saying and thinking, and he made people feel they deserved all the attention he could give them. He also appeared to be imbued with the blend of elegance and subtle desperation one saw in Fitzgerald's men. I had no clue to the source of desperation, except that he took a grim view of his last eight years—because of most of his movies and his calamitous marriage to Linda Christian, a mercenary sometime starlet to whom he paid a titanic alimony. I would later understand that his intense wish to please had damaged his life, as he accepted parts he didn't want and made concessions to women he didn't love. He loathed confrontations and did everything he could to avoid them.

Undoubtedly his sexuality complicated his life. Long afterward I was startled to hear that he was bisexual; I hadn't guessed that and Mai said she hadn't either. His name was linked with that of the actor Cesar Romero. For no logical reason I believed what had never occurred to me. Years later I came to know a man who'd had sudden sex—initiated by Power—in the men's room of an Acapulco nightclub; after that, in the bar, the actor had been particularly attentive to his wife, Linda Christian. Nor had I realized that he'd been a far-flung polygamist: Sonja Henie, Loretta Young, Janet Gaynor, the twenty-year-old Judy Garland, and Lana Turner were only a few of the women involved with him. There were rumors of affairs with Betty Grable, Gene Tierney, and Anita Ekberg. For Garland and Turner the relationships had been extremely serious, and they had hated to lose him. For a lifetime he'd dwelled at the center of others' infatuations: often he succumbed while withholding his emotions. Annabella, the French actress who was his first wife, remarked that he could hardly say no to anyone. A friend said he divided himself into separate portions and distributed them among different people.

He'd enjoyed stardom at an early age, but in midlife he felt his looks had harmed his career—by costing him substantial roles. He told Elia Kazan that for anyone who was "truly interested in the theater, it's a tragedy to be born handsome." (Kazan replied that it was worse to be born homely.) Naturally Power was conscious of his appearance, but he wasn't vain. Instead he was proud of his theatrical legacy. In his small rented house on Abingdon Road, near Kensington Court, the walls were lined with nineteenth-century posters for plays starring his great-grandfather, the Irish actor Tyrone Power, who'd enthralled audiences in Dublin, London, and the United States. Tyrone Power II (the father of the one I knew), played Shakespearean roles and in melodramas on both sides of the Atlantic, but saw little of Tyrone III—born in Cincinnati in 1914—until the father's last year. Still, the latter was supportive when the sixteen-year-old wanted to act in movies, telling him "to get to the *TOP*." The senior Power was in silent films and a few talking pictures; he died of a heart attack in his son's arms before his last one was finished.

Perhaps memories of the father's death spurred the son: as he grew older he wanted to be an important actor in the theater. *John Brown's Body,* a touring adaptation of Stephen Vincent Benét's narrative poem about the Civil War—directed by Charles Laughton and read on a bare stage with Judith Anderson and Raymond Massey in 1952—had brought Power the best reviews he'd ever had. That made him hopeful about live acting. I saw him in *The Devil's Disciple* in the fall of 1956; he'd had spectacular notices in Dublin, but no more than friendly ones in London. His performance was graceful but his immense niceness drew the emotional heat from Shaw's reprobate, and insulting others didn't seem natural to him. He was much better at being a full-fledged villain.

Throughout his career he usually underplayed—as movie actors often should in close-ups—but he was sometimes too reserved, almost passive. Henry King, one of his first directors, had advised him to hold back the emotions, even when his body was leaping all over the scenery. But he did know how to generate sexual tension: before a clinch, he told Piper Laurie, you should look into the partner's eyes, then down at the mouth, then up at the eyes again. He demanded that directors allow him to do most of his own stunts. Apart from the movies which sent him swinging bare-chested from a rope with a cutlass between his teeth or fencing with a flaming torch in one hand, or gave him such lines as "Heroism is a shallow thing if it is not rooted in wisdom" and "I'll climb so high they'll doff their hats," there were some that unleashed his authentic charm.

Before I knew Power, I thought charm was a synthetic. But his seemed inborn. To the early swashbuckling pictures—*The Mark of Zorro* and *The Black Swan*—he brought humor and a vigor that saved them from being absurd; he also seasoned those roles with a dash of parody. Although he didn't possess the acrobatic genius of Douglas Fairbanks, Sr., he displayed the quick wits essential to swordplay and tended to look amused while fighting with a hand on his hip or striding about in long swirling capes and thigh boots. In one of his most entertaining first features, *In Old Chicago,* he was what the scenarists called "a scapegrace": a joyful upstart, an exuberant seducer. He had all too few of those sprightly parts, but they indicate that he should have been given more comic roles like the young Cary Grant's: sportive, impudent, the white tie and tails instead of doublets or breastplates.

The good-heartedness that had diluted his performance in *The Devil's Disciple* had been oddly appropriate to *Jesse James* some years before; Nunnally Johnson's original script portrayed the outlaw as a an honorable rebel against the forces of industrialism, a bandit who "plays fair" with his deadly opponents. It was one of Power's choicest parts: the gentlemanly train robber who toughens up after moments of indecision. Johnson's protagonists nearly always had a dual nature; James emerges as a tarnished hero, and Power's shadowed or sunlit features emphasize the conflicts. As usual he acts mainly with his eyes, which blaze with anger or shine with pleasure when he sees his enemies or those he loves.

*Nightmare Alley,* a film noir of 1947 directed by Edmund Goulding, was Power's favorite among his movies. He had asked Zanuck to buy the novel for him, but the producer didn't want him to make it. Avid to play more complex characters than the pirates and princes who bored him, Power embraced the role of a ruthless con man whose cleverness takes him from a sleazy carnival sideshow to grand nightclubs where he convinces the rich that he can communicate with the dead as well as read the minds of the living. Power's voice becomes buttery with false sincerity and he glows when he speaks of "the spiritual life." Then he slides from one betrayal to another until he's back in the sideshow as a "geek," a drunk who bites the heads off live chickens in exchange for his daily bottle. The movie luxuriates in the downfall of those who "reached too high."

Power is wonderfully smooth and silky in his dishonesties, brimming with gusto at the height of his success, triumphant in his deceptions. As his decline begins, the actor stares into space in controlled alarm; the line between his eyebrows deepens as his despair mounts and he becomes the classic pariah of dark Forties films, a ruined cynic. The movie got very good reviews but was poorly distributed and given almost no publicity; probably the studio's executives wanted to curtail this soiled and brutal image of their glamorous star. Zanuck insisted that Power return to making some of his stickiest costume pictures, where he looks so uncomfortable that he hardly appears to be acting but is just paying a polite visit to the set.

Not until Billy Wilder's larky, sardonic *Witness for the Prosecu-*

*tion,* where Power was once again the ingratiating man with an all-too-ready smile, did he have a role that employed his talents. Wilder directed him to be subtle, restrained. The well-intentioned naïf, the beguiling drifter—rather like the deceiver of *Nightmare Alley*—is really a nimble actor, a part that Power played with a conviction absent from the movies where he had to be a courtier or conquistador. Wilder thought Power's craft was maturing and that his career was about to thrive in new realms.

After I'd known him for three months, he offered me an irresistible job. The United States Information Agency had asked him to tour Europe with a theater company of his own. He was wary of an association with the government, but was fired by the idea of a repertory troupe with choice roles for him and Mai, singly and together. I was to search for the plays, reading many untranslated French ones. At the start Mai wanted me to concentrate on Anouilh, Giraudoux, and Pirandello, and Power thought I should peruse Molnár. He decided that the company would open in New York after a year of testing in Europe and England. Aware that reading plays full-time could cloud your judgment, he said he wanted me to work like hell for eighteen hours a week, that he would pay me enough to live on so I could write the rest of the time. I was ecstatic, not only because this was like a fellowship but because I shared his and Mai's excitement about looking at international theater with a fresh eye.

Power told me he'd always longed to play Iago, the scheming monster and smiling hypocrite. It seemed right that Iago should be beguiling, even downright charming, quite like the trickster in *Nightmare Alley. Othello* would be performed each season and Mai would be Desdemona. (Because of her resounding accent— full of *v*'s for *w*'s and long *r*'s—she had not been permitted to do Shakespeare in England; Power tactfully recommended a voice coach.) *Nightmare Alley* had shown how well a miscreant's role had suited him and I hunted for others. Mai, however, wanted parts she considered "sympathetic." *Medea* would be a splendid

A. J. Liebling at the Eighth Street Bookshop

Cyril Connolly and Arthur Koestler
*©Frank Herrmann*

Elizabeth Jane Howard
*Courtesy of Colin Howard*

John Davenport

*©Frank Monaco*

Tyrone Power and Mai Zetterling during
the filming of *The Sun Also Rises*

*Courtesy of Louis Lemkow*

Donald Ogden Stewart
*©W. Suschitzky*

Ella Winter
*©W. Suschitzky*

Nora Sayre at Glyndebourne

*Photograph by Walker Evans © Walker Evans archive,
the Metropolitan Museum of Art, New York*

challenge, but otherwise she desired roles on a par with the Ibsen and Chekhov heroines she'd played: wayward and ardent, perhaps, but not dislikable. She reminded me that she had an affinity for rebels.

Promising that he wouldn't burden me with the slush pile on his desk, Power occasionally asked what I thought about certain properties, such as a movie script of John Steinbeck's *The Wayward Bus* and Peter Ustinov's version of *Benito Cereno.* (Neither seemed right for him.) He bought the film rights to Alejo Carpentier's novel *The Lost Steps* and looked forward to acting in it. He also planned to perform an adaptation of Budd Schulberg's *The Disenchanted* on Broadway and I was elated to think of him in a part based on Fitzgerald. But he acknowledged that it was difficult to play a lush without becoming terribly repetitive—and just as boring as a genuine alcoholic. Power drank little during that Kensington fall and winter, and I was later astonished to hear that—before and after that season—he sometimes hit the sauce very hard.

Ruefully he said that actors were often poor judges of material—because they tended to visualize their own parts without noticing that the rest of the script was weak or even dreadful. He spoke about a play called *A Quiet Place,* which he'd chosen without perceiving it as a whole. He portrayed a composer married to Leora Dana (a close friend of his); the characters were said to be based on Leonard Bernstein and Felicia Montealegre. The first act, full of jokes and piano music, went well on the opening night in New Haven. In the second act, which became earnest, the audience kept laughing in the wrong places. Amid mounting guffaws, Power knew that the spectators would fall apart when Dana placed a wreath on his head. Hoping to forestall that action, he seized her wrist, gazed deep into her eyes, and ad-libbed, "You must *not* do this." The bewildered actress quickly switched the wreath to her other hand and plopped it askew over his brow as bellows of laughter surged across the footlights. Getting through the remaining scenes was agonizing. The production never reached Broadway and Power said he was stricken with hepatitis soon thereafter. That experience was as demoralizing as his worst movies—including a frightful version of *Sinbad* (he'd bought up the prints and had them destroyed)—although he made it hilarious at Mai's kitchen table.

One of his foremost problems in Hollywood, he said, was having been encircled by yes-men since he was very young. He couldn't trust their opinions when they wanted him to make a particular movie, and in time he became unable to trust almost anyone, especially those in the movie industry. It seemed that he still feared being used, and in spite of his expansive social manner, caution was apparent. But he said he depended on me to be honest with him and that I must always be frank about a script or his own performances. Touched, I said I would be.

As the weeks turned into months, I pored over Aleksandr Ostrovsky (Chekhov's predecessor in the Moscow theater, whose satirical treatment of the landed gentry was attacked by the czar's censors), Arthur Adamov, the avant-garde Parisian Socialist, André Obey, whose *Rape of Lucrèce* was one of the sources for Benjamin Britten's opera, Armand Salacrou (a giant in France but unwieldy across the Channel), Marcel Achard, known for mixing burlesque and pantomime, the comedies of Marcel Aymé and André Roussin, and even Victorien Sardou, who wrote for Sarah Bernhardt. I read Lorca, Schnitzler, Büchner, and Jules Roy, and persuaded Mai to read Blixen's *Out of Africa*; she loved the idea of filming it. I was hooked on Jean Giraudoux's *Siegfried,* which did tempt them. The man who loses his memory during World War I and then suddenly recaptures his forgotten self seemed like a vibrant part for Power, blending wit and sadness with improbable hope. Because of his appetite for villainous roles I recommended Middleton and Rowley's great Jacobean tragedy *The Changeling,* where he could have been a grotesquely ugly murderer. But he rejected the play because the leading man has sex with one woman while assuming she's someone else, and he said he couldn't possibly believe that you wouldn't know who you were in bed with. Over Mai's tall glasses of Russian tea, smoking long Turkish cigarettes, the three of us discussed one play after another and how each might be directed. In the decade that followed, many of the plays I'd selected would be translated and produced; most are familiar now, but they were discoveries then.

Mai built a strong and playful community around her, as she would throughout her life. Although she was a fairly neglectful mother—she'd had children too young, when she didn't want them—she had a talent for creating a tribe, and she was able to give others a sense of security that she couldn't quite fashion for herself. I can't explain this: I know only that the nourishing atmosphere around her seemed more fortifying for her friends than it was for her or the children. Productivity and mutual support were the keystones, the air was charged with encouragement. Kensington Court was a close temporary family: Mai and Power seemed like delightful older relatives, not parental but somewhat like guardians. (Power wanted to meet the young men I went out with, though Mai shrank from the thought of strangers in her home.) Louis Lemkow, Mai's son, became the best kid brother I'd never had—as I told him years afterward, when he was the vice president of the University of Barcelona.

In childhood Louis went to London's French Lycée, scrupulously followed the wars in Algeria and Cyprus, relished Jacques Cousteau's *The Silent World* and tried out his frogman flippers in the bathtub, and practiced an exultant atheism, stating that he could "believe in germs but not God." Informed that certain phenomena existed unseen, he laughed and said, "Show me God under a microscope!" Told by a teacher that "God is everywhere," Louis retorted, "Then I can punch him in the belly" and proceeded to belt the air with both fists.

His elder sister Etienne was a deeply troubled child, given to frantic eruptions and great fogs of depression that seemed painfully adult for an eleven-year-old. But she also had humor and shrewdness and she liked to throw her seniors off balance. Mai and I took her to a film of the Bolshoi Ballet's *Romeo and Juliet*; the ending displeased her but she was intrigued that Juliet was fourteen and Romeo was probably about the same age. She said, "I bet they wouldn't have known what to do after they were married." We kept our faces blank. "But in Siam they get married even younger—and I bet *they* know what to do." We shook with the laughter she often provoked. Her preferred Sunday treat occurred at the London Zoo, where you could be photographed with another person when both were entwined by a docile boa constrictor: her favorite boa-mate was Power. In her early twenties she would be diagnosed as a borderline schizophrenic, but I never forgot the lively mind that surfaced amid the dejections.

Shortly before Christmas, Mai and Power appeared in Strindberg's *Miss Julie* on live television. I was impressed; as usual she excelled at rapid mood swings and he made the valet both likable and menacing without losing the irony. On the afternoon of December 24, when I thought Flat Seven was empty, I heard odd noises in the living room and flung the door open, switching on the lights. Flat on the carpet, lying on their stomachs and partly hidden under the piano, Power and Arthur, his chauffeur, were secretly installing a sixteen-millimeter movie projector, a surprise gift for Mai. (In those years before cassettes, a first-rate home projector was a luxury, and she had yearned for one.)

Mai organized—no, directed—Christmas day with such gusto

that she was greatly teased by Power: "Well, Nora! She says *breakfast* at *ten* and *lunch* at *three* and presents *after* lunch. Now what can we do to turn it all upside down?" He wouldn't wait for the presents because he was so eager to amaze her with his own. So we tore open all our packages right after breakfast while the children ran wild. Power gave me a very fine Parker pen so that ink wouldn't leak all over my fingers (as it did from my cheap fountain pens), Mai's gift was a bright red leather writing case, Liebling sent two Roman coins—Hadrian, because I'd loved visiting his villa, and Claudius, looking quite like my favorite Frenchman, Gérard Philipe—and the *New Statesman* staff delivered a jar of Greek honey, said to be the original ambrosia.

For our holiday banquet Power had requested a magnificent sirloin, hominy grits from Harrods, hearts of palm; in a tall pitcher he mixed champagne and Guinness for Black Velvets. Ted Richmond, Power's partner in Copa Productions, and Richmond's anxious wife joined us at the table. Richmond refused garlic salad dressing "because it's un-Californian." His wife, after admiring Mai's antique wine glasses, said she could never have any like that since her guests usually broke things (drunk, I supposed); if they couldn't replace them, they would be wretched and that would mean she was a bad hostess. When we were gloriously stuffed, Power ran the new projector and showed us one of Mai's first Swedish pictures, *Sunshine Follows the Rain,* a outdoor melodrama where she elopes with a gypsy fiddler, and *Nightmare Alley,* my first glimpse of him basking in wickedness.

That Christmas was enhanced by the happiness of Mai and Power; after everyone had gone, she told me she'd never felt like this in her thirty-one years. That evening she didn't scoff at happiness, and I felt fortunate to be in their magnetic field. Certainly I was romantic on their behalf, and when they swore they would never marry, that sounded like a way of prolonging love, of keeping them even more romantic. Their affair, the theater company, my own growing confidence in work and life seemed to assure a sparkling future. Within a year they would part, I would be married to a man I hadn't yet met, in eighteen months each of them would remarry, and Power would die in less than two years. Yet I think that day made us feel that further rewards were in store for us—Mai and I agreed about that.

Jean Anouilh's plays had captivated English audiences for more than a decade. Calling himself a comic misanthrope, the playwright divided his works into "Pièces Roses" (his lightest creations, which are nonetheless quite cynical) and "Pièces Noirs," dark tragicomedies which echo his belief that the human animal is equally "inconsolable and gay." Some of his male characters are witty, bitter ex-romantics, demoralized because love doesn't last; they think decency is doomed in a foul world. Many of his heroines are engaging truth-tellers: young women who have passed through horrors but remain uncorruptible, honest while surrounded by lies.

Anouilh's *Antigone, Ring Around the Moon, The Lark, The Waltz of the Toreadors,* and many others had lengthy runs in London. Mai had long wanted to perform *La Sauvage*, an early noir (clumsily translated as *Restless Heart*), where the protagonist—raised in a squalid seaside café by repulsive, avaricious parents—is loved by a wealthy composer who aims to rescue her from a humiliating existence. Although she loves him, she rejects the luxury and stability he offers because she can't dwell in a milieu where suffering isn't acknowledged. It's as though Cinderella abandoned the Prince—a deed that lacerates her.

After the curtain rises on a ghastly little café orchestra, with its squeaky violins and a sick cello, the early scenes shimmer with Anouilh's most pessimistic charm. But on a first reading I saw that the third act repeated parts of the second, and the angry heroine appeared to be creating many of her own problems. I was sure that wasn't Anouilh's intention, since she was meant to be appealing. But the character seemed to have put him in a double bind: as she hurls her lover's books on his library floor, gets her father drunk and makes him sing obscene songs, and cherishes her own pain. The play asks: why does she walk out on the desirable man she loves? But the playwright didn't answer that question. When I told Mai that I thought the young woman was perverse, she was upset and denied it vehemently. (Later I learned that she thought "perverse" meant homosexual; of a couple of unhappy youthful lesbian encounters, she said "I was perverse," meaning "perverted.") Still, she managed to make the tempestuous waif heroic, mating her disbelief in security—a Zetterling credo—with a defiance of all conventions; in the final scene she sails out into the world as a solitary and jubilant survivor. The quest for freedom would be a recurrent theme in the films Mai directed in the Sixties and thereafter, and in her fiction.

The role of the rich lover was not well cast, since it wasn't substantial enough to attract an actor of Paul Scofield's stature (he turned it down). But Donald Pleasence as a greedy, sniveling sot and Peter Bull as a caustic commentator were at their melancholy best. Superb reviews piled up as *La Sauvage* went on tour. In his Daimler, Power whirled his friends Kurt Kasznar and Leora Dana and me down to Brighton, where we were dazzled by Mai's performance. Next day, during a seafood lunch—Power insisted on ordering a mystifying black hors d'oeuvre for us called lava bread, which tasted like fish roe but was actually seaweed—we rejoiced in Mai's immediate future. In Brighton the play was sold out in one day; hundreds were turned away from the box office. The out-of-town notices continued to be excellent and *La Sauvage* looked like a milestone in her career. Surely the production would go to Broadway. Still, we heard that a representative of the Theatre Guild, who had liked it very much, said that the contempt for money might make it unsuitable for New York.

Mai's tour was scheduled to last only a few weeks, but it

dragged on because of a theater strike in London. Louis and I ran
the household while she was on the road, distributing the pay
packets she sent. The number of employees kept increasing: a benign and patient Oxford graduate I'd hired to tutor Etienne—
she pretended she couldn't read, but he soon got her to do so
while he grappled with her sexual fantasies about him—two
chars, because one couldn't stoop and the other couldn't lift, a
voluptuous seventeen-year-old Swedish au pair (often joined by
her Belgian boyfriend, training as a caterer, who served elaborate
dinners to us), Nora-the-cook, who fed the children and hosted a
perpetual coffee party in the kitchen, and Mrs. Lillian Ruddy,
Power's devoted housekeeper, who checked in and cast a stern
eye on the amounts of sugar, Nescafé, butter, and tea that some
of the others ordered and took home. One of Mai's friends said
that life at Flat Seven mingled characters from Turgenev and
Chekhov: there was the actress mother, the handsome young
tutor, a slew of servants, the ironic doctor who was also a family
friend, and the mysterious house guest—me.

Mai returned for one or two nights a week, pale with exhaustion, worried that the production was rusting during the long
tour. Wheeling out the new projector, Power chose movies to
cheer her: Chaplin, Harold Lloyd, *Rock Around the Clock,* and a
documentary on Hieronymus Bosch. He also brought armloads
of Linda Christian's clothing to Kensington Court, exasperated
that she kept parking her sumptuous wardrobe in his house
while she pursued a couple of titled Englishmen, whom he called
"targets for tonight." He told me to keep any garments I liked
and give the rest to the refugees from the Hungarian Revolution
of 1956. Most of the Christian costumes were too small for me,
but I did acquire a lovely mauve silk jacket and a long white lace
skirt. Power said that early in their marriage he'd realized that
she cared for almost nothing but clothes—and money. Annabella, his first wife, came to dinner one night. She and Mai, who
hadn't met, were both wearing black jersey scoop-neck tops and

white wool skirts, each embroidered with metallic threads: one
in gold, one in silver. Uneasy laughter. Annabella seemed a warm
and considerate person, but all three were tense and upright, extremely formal, and Mai threw up right after dinner.

Soon afterward Power handed me Peter Viertel's script of *The
Sun Also Rises,* commissioned by Darryl Zanuck. I thought it a
very skillful translation; much of the dialogue came straight from
Hemingway's novel. Power didn't want to be away from Mai,
since they would also be separated while he made *Witness for the
Prosecution.* But he finally and reluctantly went off to play Jake
Barnes. I was more enthusiastic about the film-to-be than he was,
though I should have known he wasn't a Hemingway character.
Nor did it occur to me then that Power—now forty-three—was
too old for the part. So were several actors chosen to play the
young male carousers of the Twenties—Errol Flynn and Eddie
Albert were almost fifty—and I was horrified that the wooden
Mel Ferrer was signed for Robert Cohn.

All the casting was Zanuck's; after securing Power, he selected
Henry King, a prolific director who was too conventional to develop a personal style and was known for slow pacing. He had
directed Power's father in a silent movie called *Fury.* As a junior
actor, the son had contacted King, who starred him in *Lloyd's of
London,* Power's first box-office smash. Then he would make ten
more pictures with King, many of them tedious.

*La Sauvage,* still awaiting a London theater, closed for two
weeks. For Mai's birthday, Power sent her a first-class air ticket
to Morelia, Mexico, where much of *The Sun Also Rises* was being
shot. As her small plane landed in a field, he met her with a
Mariachi band. She didn't know that brief flings usually accompanied his major affairs, nor that a young Mexican woman, an
extra, was his girlfriend during the filming—when he seemed
totally focused on Mai. (For his lovers, what appeared to be
single-mindedness was part of his charm.) Flynn, cast as Mike
Campbell, was soaking up gallons of tequila. Ava Gardner (Lady

Brett) was swilling dry martinis as well as tequila and was often late for her scenes. Mai thought Gardner hated acting or the camera—or both, that she dreaded even the prospect of performing. Robert Evans, recently an executive in the clothing industry and a future Paramount producer, was a dumbfounding choice for the brilliant young matador. As he paraded across the bullring, the crowd of hundreds of Mexican extras exploded with laughter; the scene had to be reshot and the assistant director kept imploring them not to whoop or jeer at Evans's way of walking and his awkward appearance in the bullfighter's costume. Power and Viertel, the screenwriter, urged Zanuck and King to drop him, but they loftily refused. When the movie was released, Zanuck promoted Evans as a successor to Rudolph Valentino.

Jean Anouilh came from France to the London dress rehearsal of *La Sauvage* and was very pleased with what he saw. He told Mai he approved of her reinterpretation of the ending: when the heroine leaves her lover on a positive note. (To her astonishment he said he didn't like sad plays.) The director reasonably feared that the cast would be creaky after some three months on the road and a fortnight of nonperformance. So he called for two full run-throughs on the very day of the opening. That night was a predictable disaster: the actors, infected with the director's nervousness, were also drooping with fatigue, while Mai flung herself around the stage in an effort to energize them; she didn't over-act, but she was far too manic for the character. The play's weaknesses were harshly exposed: the repetitive third act, the heroine's contradictory nature—she seemed destructive to no purpose, even quite crazed in several scenes—and *La Sauvage* appeared muddled as it hadn't before. It was the first time I'd seen a production so violently altered that the material itself seemed to have changed. Mai was deeply depressed afterward; she demanded honest responses from her friends and we gave them, staying up until four in the morning, pouring glasses of champagne for her which she hardly touched.

I was told that the second night was transcendent, but after the first night the reviews were devastating, and the play lasted only a few weeks. Mai took it bravely, but it seemed like a bad omen for Giraudoux's *Ondine,* which she and Power planned for a limited run in London; later it would be part of the repertory season. So would Chekhov's *Platonov,* his guilt-ravaged Don Juan pursued by clamorous women. That was the part that excited Power most of all; it was said to be Chekhov's first play, and Power hoped that Tyrone Guthrie might direct it. But after *La Sauvage* closed, the lash of failure when success seemed certain was demoralizing for all of us, from Mrs. Ruddy to the children.

*The Sun Also Rises* inspired a rave from *Time,* and Power was praised in *The Herald Tribune.* His performance was thoughtful and sensitive as his eyes widened or narrowed while Brett chased other men. In the novel Jake Barnes is a robust character, a lively, ironic foreign correspondent who likes Paris and good meals, hiking and fishing. But in the movie he's merely a sad spectator, and Power's role mainly consists of staring silently at Ava Gardner. The fine script I'd read had been repeatedly rewritten, and the scene where Barnes is told that he'll be impotent is stilted and embarrassing, accompanied by haunting music. Gardner had none of the class her part required, grinning broadly when pleased or squealing when upset. Zanuck and Viertel had eliminated the novel's anti-Semitic lines, so the group's verbal abuse of Robert Cohn isn't bigoted; they simply find him irritating (which indeed Mel Ferrer is).

For much of the movie Flynn appears as a drunk playing a drunk, but he achieves a suave and acrid dignity toward the end, and he got the best reviews of anyone in the picture. The last lines, when Brett says, "Oh darling, there must be an answer for us somewhere," and Barnes replies, "I'm sure there is," made me think of dildos. Hemingway had already denounced the revised script. There was no vitality in a film that should have seethed with the passions of expatriate revelers and a town celebrating its bulls and matadors. I was too disappointed to tell Power what I thought, but he—who volunteered that the movie hadn't turned out as he'd wished—stressed that it brought him the first good review he'd ever had in *Time*. (He must have forgotten that James Agee had liked *Nightmare Alley*.) Maybe he didn't want to criticize Zanuck and King, who had shaped so much of his career— the career he had wanted to change.

Mai flew to Los Angeles to visit Power while he was making *Witness for the Prosecution*. His rapport with Billy Wilder was heartening for him: the director respected him as an actor, appreciated his intelligence and his humor. Later Power told me that it had been difficult to work with his co-star, Marlene Dietrich, because of a healed-over slit in her scalp; he said the edges were held together by a metal clamp which drew the skin up tightly on her face, under a blond wig. This was an instant face-lift and he'd had to handle her very carefully to avoid giving her pain. She was smitten with him—as she often was with her leading men— and so was Charles Laughton, the ugly gay man who adored handsome ones. Wilder remembered that "everyone had a crush" on Power, that even for a heterosexual "it was impossible to be totally impervious to that kind of charm."

In Los Angeles Mai was eager to discuss the European repertory tour that she and Power had planned. But she found him distant, and she was hurt and bewildered. I'd asked her to call my father, who was staying in Santa Monica and writing a treatment for a movie Humphrey Bogart didn't live to make, to give him news of me. They had never met, but the next thing I heard was that Mai had taken off with him at 2:00 A.M. on one of his excursions to see the ceremonial dances of the Hopi Indians in Arizona. (He had many friends among the Hopis and used to drive carloads of their corn to trade with the Navajos in New Mexico. Perhaps his foremost religious experience occurred during a Hopi rain dance: he was terrifically impressed by the ensuing cloudburst and a tremendous electrical blackout.) After a grueling day on the road in my father's rickety old Studebaker, they camped out for a week in the hills, amid red rocks and sage-brush, where snakes were seen as messengers who took the Hopis' prayers to Mother Earth. He and Mai watched daylong kachina dances by masked men dressed as demigods: the dancers and their Hopi audience believed they had temporarily become ancestral spirits.

My father complimented Mai on her "truly Viking" stomach for adventure. She later said that expedition was a turning point in her life, that the experience had given her the courage to become a director. She also told me that my father had remarked that he'd always wanted to see a Lapp festival in Jokkmokk in the Arctic Circle. (He intended to write a "Letter from Lapland" for *The New Yorker*, but didn't get there.) That, she said, eventually gave her the idea for her first documentary, shot in Lapland. So the Hopi excursion sent her to a frozen landscape filled with reindeer, elk, and nomads whose lives were much like those of their ancestors of a thousand years before. Her love of the wilderness would lead to documentaries in Iceland and Greenland, where the Eskimos fascinated her as much as the gypsies she would film in the South of France.

In a few years Mai lost the desire to act, then seemed to dislike acting altogether: she said it demanded passivity. Many changes lay ahead for her, more than she or her friends could foresee. She was not yet the passionate feminist she would become in the Sixties. The movies she directed in Sweden flatter neither sex, and both are guilty of hypocrisy. In her first feature films—*Loving Couples, Night Games, The Girls*—most of the men are destructive or ineffectual, but she was often harder on the women, making them look ridiculous if they aren't strong and independent. She mocked timid or conventional women while she portrayed female monsters with gusto: creatures who excel at de-grading others. Themes of of incest and castration, wretched marriages, love gone wrong, and madness surge through her films in the midst of an uneasy eroticism. Her Freudian approach to her characters—as they masturbate, vomit, writhe in pain or sickness, tear their clothes, and pick their noses—can seem naive. (I doubt if she had read much Freud, but his views pervaded the world she knew.) Yet her spellbinding visual talents are revealed in each scene, especially when she explores women's fantasies of what they want or what they fear, the daydreams and nightmares of questing heroines.

Her sensuous imagery dwells on what she found beautiful: masked figures in gondolas gliding through Venetian canals; a white dove released from a dark blue scarf; a butterfly at a win-dow; smoke rising from big torches, reflections in water. She loved white: white ceilings, nightgowns, lilies and white lilacs, white lace curtains, birds, clothing on a line, birch trees, winter sun, snowy landscapes. Grim images are also plentiful, as when a woman gives a costume party timed to the birth of her (stillborn) baby—a jazz band accompanies her labor—or a man shouts as he pounds on the wall of a madhouse, or when there's a rape in a brothel. In a sideshow a shackled man hangs upside down near glass jars filled with organs; a familiar face is seen in a distorting mirror.

Mai's appetite for the grotesque—even the gruesome—may have sprung from a conviction that ugliness is a reality that many people shrink from facing but must be made to confront. Maybe she hoped to shock the repressive Nordic society she was raised in—although it was no longer repressive. For a festival program of *Night Games,* she wrote, "I believe you can only come to a pos-itive view of things by passing through innumerable negative views"—even so, some spectators called her films pornographic. Her two short novels and a book of stories, published between 1966 and 1976, are awash with repellent liquids: runny egg yolks, the putrid juice of a rotten mushroom, streams of piss and diarrhea, and the puking hardly stops. Her own highly personal humor—which welled up when she told stories about what happened yesterday or years ago—was scarce in her movies and fiction, where she tended toward Rabelaisian farce.

Long after Kensington Court I wasn't surprised by the vehemence of her writing, but I was puzzled by the disgust for the body, and I didn't understand it—because she spoke of sex with such pleasure. Still, her reflexes had been developed in Calvinist Scandinavia, and like Ingmar Bergman she rebelled against the blistering chill of a culture which could inhibit or unhinge its freer spirits. Perhaps they felt that suppressed emotions could breed corruption and cruelty. In their land, healthy lust had sometimes been regarded as sordid and unnatural, and their films expressed the torments of people who felt cheated of normality. Strindbergian terrors and hallucinations frequently besiege their characters. Mai moved in 1959 to the English countryside, later to an isolated spot in the South of France; she wasn't much in touch with the liberations of the Sixties, and didn't seem to know that repression had faded. So she continued to challenge the weakening custodians of morality. An ebullient pagan, she detested Christianity; two of her favorite directors, Buñuel and Fellini, derided the Church. (Her Siamese cat was named Fellina 8½.) Surrealism, metaphysics, even mysticism absorbed her as she grew older, and although she understood that life was not predictable, she often wished it could be.

Mai came back to London from Hollywood very anxious about her relations with Power, who certainly appeared to be withdrawing from her. A month later, when I was in New York, he introduced me to Debbie Minardos, a dark-haired young Mississippian only two years older than myself. She was given to loud screams of laughter, and she liked to repeat a favorite joke about elephant shit (I've forgotten the punch line). She also gushed about Elvis Presley, whom she said she had dated. She came on as a vivacious airhead, but I could see that she was tough.

Power cautiously asked me to tell Mai about Debbie, but I said that wasn't the role of a friend and he hastily agreed. It seemed that Mai's many refusals to compromise—in personal or professional life—had discomfited him. He spoke of her artistry with tremendous admiration, but admitted that he found her overwhelming, too demanding, and it appeared that he'd become rather afraid of her. Sadly I thought of how often she spoke proudly of her independence—yet was more dependent on the men in her life than any woman I knew. And I sensed that this affectionate man discouraged nothing but intimacy. Mai had leaped over the barriers he'd erected, and I mourned the parting from Power not only for her sake but because I had idealized them as a couple: I'd thought they would endure. The end of their affair made me skeptical about continuity: if those two could break up, what chance did any of us have? My naïveté and my romanticism didn't fade, but my confidence in couples did.

At a buffet dinner at Power's small Park Avenue penthouse, where guests were invited to see NBC's seventy-fifth anniversary tribute to Standard Oil of New Jersey, hosted by Power, I heard Debbie tell the elephant joke twice. Mike Todd didn't seem to appreciate it. His wife Elizabeth Taylor had been discussing diets at length in another room; suddenly her beautiful eyes widened and she cried, "Mike's *eating* again! I can *tell!*" She rushed to his side and tried to snatch a big drumstick from his paw, but he growled merrily and vowed to eat all of it—and her, too.

Power—who left the party to narrate the show and came back right afterward—told me how appalled he'd been by *West Side Story,* which had just opened; he said a stageful of dancing delinquents was abhorrent, it was like making a musical about syphilis or gonorrhea. Art Buchwald, the Paris columnist for *The Herald*

*Tribune,* ambled around the living room saying hello twice; as I heard him chanting "Hello, hello" to yet another pair, I wondered how anyone could be so relentlessly cheerful. (Six years later he was hospitalized with clinical depression, an affliction of many humorists.) Someone described the British actor who drove on the left side of Hollywood roads, shouting, "Don't Americans know the traffic laws!"

After we'd watched NBC—my first glimpse of color TV—where Power had to laud petroleum between listless numbers featuring such performers as Jane Powell ("the girl of today"), I noticed that Power was looking his very best. His luster wasn't diminished even when uttering lines like "Most of the rubber we use doesn't come from trees, but from petroleum." Maybe this really was the life that suited him—more than the theater, more than the soul-searching Mai required. And yet he'd appeared to be so happy in London: with her. Was that acting? Perhaps—on the part of a man who went on wanting to please. I was enjoying myself as I listened to the show-business jokes in his New York home, but the whole evening seemed a solar distance away from the bonds of Kensington Court, the joyful plans and the hopes for the future.

In my early twenties I knew little about loss; I thought the fluid world I inhabited was self-renewing, and I didn't expect individuals who were important to me to disappear. For me death was an abstraction—as it is to most of the young. The people who had intrigued or influenced me would live in my memory, and I could hardly imagine a time when I couldn't sit down or stroll along a street with them while hearing the enthralling things they had to say.

Tyrone Power died just after fencing with George Sanders on a movie set in Spain, filming *Solomon and Sheba* in 1958. I'd been told that he was very depressed: he'd slid back into the kind of movie and marriage that he'd tried so hard to escape; swamps and whirlpools had awaited him. He was forty-four when his heart stopped. Long afterward I was told by our London doctor that he'd requested amphetamine shots, which were popular in the British backstage community. Our doctor had refused, warning of dangers to the heart, but Power had found a feel-good doctor. At his funeral in Hollywood his widow sat by the open coffin, holding his dead hand while an organ played "I'll Be Loving You Always." Their son was born two months later.

Thirty-six years afterward Mai was stricken with pancreatic cancer, a death sentence she would not accept. Dying, she outlined a new novel, *Black Snow, White Rain,* finished writing half of a short book on Carl Dreyer's *Passion of Joan of Arc,* and planned the filming of her novel *Bird of Passage.* After struggling to stay alive and enduring past her doctors' predictions, she asked to hear Schubert's late Quartet in G Major on the last day of her life in 1994. Following Kensington Court she had directed six feature films and many short ones and written four books. In her final decade she'd owned a romantic semi-ruin in the South of France: a seventeenth-century monastery which was later a silk factory and then the home of a nineteenth-century coal baron. Relatives and friends came from several countries to bury her ashes under a tall tree near grape vines, lavender, olives, and herb gardens. At the beginning of a long July sunset, each of us scattered a shovelful of dirt on top of the ashes: then, in keeping with a Scandinavian custom, everyone poured a glass of wine onto the fresh earth. From her grave we could see Mont Blanc.

# V.

My country's anti-Communist crusade inspired quips about "un-British activities" in London, where many thought the American chastisement of left-wingers was absurd. When President Eisenhower deferred to the red-hunters, his administration was disparaged in England, and I heard the White House called "the tomb of the well-known soldier." I had a great deal to learn about the domestic Cold War; as a student I'd scarcely read the newspapers, and neither my background nor my teachers had introduced me to the central issues. Gradually I found I needed to examine some recent American history—as I had not before. It would take quite a few years to fill many gaps, but my time in London helped to clarify what was happening at home, the fears and hatreds that were raging through the landscape I'd left behind.

Growing up in Manhattan I'd had no acquaintance with the American Left; my parents and their friends were largely apolitical. Most were the fairly cynical heirs of H. L. Mencken, the great editorial arsonist who had put his torch to middle-class values, who despised the New Deal and referred to Karl Marx as "the philosopher out of the gutter." As Edmund Wilson observed,

Mencken had also schooled the generation of the jazz age "to think of politics as an obscene farce," and his admirers ridiculed leftists of the Thirties for thinking that social progress was possible. A distinct but non-punitive anti-Communism permeated my parents' world of New York writers. But although they didn't care for the ideas of radicals or Communists, they were disgusted by the political investigations of the Fifties, and most felt badly about individuals who landed on the blacklist. Meanwhile quite a few of those who were barred from working in Hollywood or at our universities went abroad in search of employment.

In London the spectrum of American political exiles included the family of a college friend. In their living room I encountered some of the men and women who had been fired for their politics, which had repelled and mystified millions of my compatriots. By the mid-Fifties most left-wingers had traveled far from the ideological strife of the Thirties; many had already devoted about five years to their legal problems and to finding stopgap jobs.

Delighted to see other Americans when London was still new to me, I was soon spending most of my Sunday afternoons at 103 Frognal. That vast Georgian house high on a hill in Hampstead echoed with the preoccupations of the screenwriter Donald Ogden Stewart and journalist Ella Winter, who had been married to the social critic Lincoln Steffens before DOS, as Stewart was often called. Blacklisted writers and film-makers who, like DOS, had been deprived of their passports by the State Department joined the British socialists and artists who flocked to Frognal every week.

The house had been the home of British Prime Minister Ramsay MacDonald, and the street was named for the frogs which had filled its former swamps. From the mid-Fifties onward, numerous Americans gathered at Frognal to reminisce about a lifetime on the Left, to compare their experiences with

the FBI, to whoop in DOS's gentle deadpan presence at his sting-
ing jokes, to yell when Ella—filling teacups from a great height
—poured hot water into the laps or crotches of her seated guests.

Amid the shouts of laughter and the cries of the scalded, between bursts of music from records just arrived from New York,
such as *Damn Yankees,* and the barks of Ella's frantic miniature
poodle or the sobs of small children bewildered by the commotion, the ideas of those who had been called un-American did
emerge. The Sundays were festive, often hilarious: you didn't
hear political analysis over the teapot. Sometimes you could
hardly hear anything: while early recordings of Joe Hill or tapes
of animal noises (brought from Africa by one of Ella's young protégés) were playing at full volume. Yet there was a powerful sense
of community. I began to understand that the old American Left
was an intimate extended family: over the decades, most had not
only worked together, they'd spent their free time with one another, rented rooms to each other, raised their children together,
and—by the time I met them—suffered together. They had had
their differences—about how to aid the San Francisco longshoremen during the strike of 1934, about how to gather more money
for medical supplies for the Spanish Loyalists—but cohesion was
based on an assumption that commitments were still shared.
That gave them a continuity which seemed to be heartening in
their blacklist years. So did shared antipathies: they agreed with
a *New Statesman* editor who said Franco's worst mistake was not
shooting Arthur Koestler.

Among the Frognal visitors were independent radicals, ex-
Communists, and authentic liberals; naturally they couldn't con-
cur on every point. But in that house I was first exposed to those
who felt a responsibility for the character of their own society.
Their government or their former employers had asked them to
disown their beliefs or to apologize for them; they had not coop-
erated. But some were still sorting out the accusations leveled
against them; after they'd trudged through forests of anger and

depression, they were still amazed at the notion of their alleged guilt.

As many historians have noted, the themes of the Cold War sprang to national attention through the investigations of the film industry, and the 1947 firings in Hollywood set a pattern that would be followed in professions throughout the country. At Frognal the recent survivors were reassessing the upheavals which had marooned them on a safe but remote reef. Or fairly safe: long afterward I read my hosts' FBI files and discovered how closely they were watched even in Hampstead.

Subsequently I became engrossed by the effects of the Cold War at home—especially the blacklist—and set out to learn about the impact on American movie-making. I questioned the survivors and watched dozens of old films. During the New Deal there had been a handful of movies about "progressive" subjects, such as poverty and tenant farming, while businessmen and landlords often appeared as villains. And a wave of anti-fascist pictures went into production right after Pearl Harbor was bombed. Immediately after World War II, some producers encouraged films that explored current social questions, such as the anti-Semitism examined in *Crossfire* and *Gentleman's Agreement* or the predicaments of returning veterans in *The Best Years of Our Lives*. With an eye on best-selling books, the producers were correct in expecting the topical to be profitable. Therefore until late in 1947 the screenwriters of the Left were able to incorporate some mild versions of their views into their scripts. But opportunities were limited because the studio executives felt that the public disliked "messages" and because writers weren't in charge of content: the producers were totally in control of the final screeenplays.

Writers had been considered alien and suspect beings in Hollywood since the Thirties, partly because many of them came from the East. The structure of the industry kept them in quarantine: isolated in their offices, unwelcome on the set. Producer Jack Warner defined writers as "schmucks with Underwoods." At Columbia all the lights were switched off at 7:30 because Harry Cohn, the head of the studio, thought writers who worked late were either drunk or lazy, so there was no point in wasting electricity. Cecil B. De Mille, convinced that "Pretty writing can ruin a picture," had also declared, "God protect me from the writer who wants to write." MGM producer Irving Thalberg was said to have described the writer as "a necessary evil." Screenwriters were constantly replaced: often a whole series of them worked on the same script, and frequently a writer would discover that several others had been secretly assigned to the same project at the same time. Yet although writers were treated as near-irrelevancies, the executives feared their influence. The issue was economic rather than political: writers were thought to be poor judges of what would be commercial.

Contrary to the insistence of the House Committee on Un-American Activities that postwar movies were seething with Communist propaganda, even writers who were Communists knew it was impossible to make left-wing films. Still, some were excited by the idea of writing egalitarian material which would be seen by a large audience. But at most they could advance "democratic" themes: they wrote pictures upholding equality or opposing oppression—in a tone that was tailored to the realities of the movie business, where entertainment was always the priority. So the aims of the Left were usually modest: to portray an intelligent black character or the erosions of unemployment, or even (although rarely) a woman who earned her own living.

Some conveyed sympathy for the labor movement, others depicted the bravery of those who battled fascism abroad. Occasionally one of the Marxists wrote a script that seemed to condemn the American way of life or the corruptions of our government, but it was revised by the producers to deflect any controversy. Very few films were as radical as *Body and Soul* (written by Abraham Polonsky and directed by Robert Rossen) or Polonsky's *Force of Evil,* which dissected the consequences of craving much more money than one needs—in a culture that increases the appetite for opulence. Before he was blacklisted, Polonsky wrote brilliantly pessimistic movies charged with sufficient violence to appeal to popular tastes, and they were concerned with working people at a time when Hollywood concentrated on the middle class.

The content of movies was a pivotal issue in the Committee's hearings of 1947. *Mission to Moscow* (1943) and *Song of Russia* (1944) were gargantuan mash notes to our wartime ally; both were considered patriotic during the war and branded as subversive a few years afterward. Committee members suspected that the Roosevelt administration had pressured the studios to make them, though the producers denied it. *Mission to Moscow,* based on the memoirs of Joseph Davies, ambassador to Russia from 1936 to 1938, claimed that the defendants in the Moscow trials were guilty (which Davies believed), showed Stalin as a benign figure, and neglected to mention Communism.

*Song of Russia,* initially intended as a tribute to the Russian resistance, was a semi-musical which suggested that scorching the earth was a tuneful procedure: happy peasants sang and danced when they weren't fighting the Germans and the film bypassed the Nazi-Soviet pact. The movie was written by two Communists—Richard Collins, who later gave twenty-three names to the Committee, and Paul Jarrico, who was blacklisted after Collins and others named him—but they were not allowed to show that the joyful peasants worked on a collective farm and they had to cut the word "community" from their script. In an early shot, Robert Taylor conducted our national anthem and the scene dissolved from New York to Moscow, where a Soviet band continued "The Star-Spangled Banner" beneath a hammer and sickle. Laslo Benedek, the assistant producer, told me that he was accused of conspiring to impel American audiences to rise for their anthem and to remain standing in the presence of the red flag while the soundtrack switched to the Russian anthem.

Both movies were unintentionally comic, but the Committee cited them as evidence that Roosevelt and Hollywood were Stalin's dupes. Ginger Rogers's mother, employed by RKO to scrutinize scripts for Communist dogma, testified at length. Committee members also heard right-wing witnesses describing un-American moments in *The Best Years of Our Lives,* where a bank was reluctant to give a veteran a G.I. loan, and in Clifford Odets's screenplay for *Deadline at Dawn,* where Lela Rogers detected Communist inspiration in a joke which implied that it was a crime not to be a success. Toward the end of the hearings, Committee chairman J. Parnell Thomas said the Committee would produce "an extensive study" of Communist propaganda in motion pictures, but that document never appeared.

In truth Hollywood's overwhelming attraction for the Committee was its celebrities: the investigators had a fixation on the famous. Although the public hardly knew the names of writers or directors, the word *Hollywood* conferred a kind of royalty—which meant dazzling publicity for the Committee. For Mississippi Congressman John Rankin, who had reactivated the Committee in 1945, Jews and Communists were barely distinguishable—and much of the power in Hollywood was Jewish. (Although the percentage of Jews in the American Communist Party is uncertain, some historians have estimated that during the Thirties and Forties about half the membership was Jewish.) But the Congressman may not have realized that most of the Jews who owned the studios were staunch anti-Communists. Rankin said in 1945 that those who were plotting to "overthrow" the government had their "headquarters in Hollywood," which was "the greatest hotbed of subversive activities in the United States." To him, Communism and Judaism were the same, and he explained to the Congress that "Communism is older than Christianity. . . .

It hounded and persecuted the Savior during his earthly ministry, inspired his crucifixion, derided him in his dying agony, and then gambled for his garments at the foot of the cross." He added that "alien-minded Communistic enemies of Christianity and their stooges" were trying to seize control of the media, including "the radio. Listen to their lying broadcasts in broken English and you can almost smell them."

J. Parnell Thomas, who became chairman of the Committee in 1946, did not share the Mississippian's obsession with Jews, though the anti-Communist crusade continued to resound with anti-Semitism. Like his colleagues, Thomas was intent on equating the New Deal with Communism and in persuading voters that Truman was perpetuating the New Deal (when he was actually retreating from its policies). And Hollywood was as rich in admirers of the New Deal as it was in Jews. By 1951—after Thomas had been jailed for payroll padding—the Committee members were also stimulated by knowing that the Hollywood Left had collected large sums for such causes as Russian War Relief, refugees from fascist countries, and the more radical unions. And the investigators were well aware that contributions to some front groups benefited the American Communist Party. By that time, many citizens were convinced that our movies were riddled with Communist doctrine.

Between the Sundays at Frognal, I thought about how the guests were still vilified in their own land. Why did the putative victors—right-wingers and anti-Communist liberals—still detest those who had been fired, ostracized, even jailed and deported? As I went with them to new American movies like *Marty* and *The Man with the Golden Arm,* or heard them describing the Hollywood producers' hostility toward the Screen Writers Guild or the feuds between Louis B. Mayer and Irving Thalberg at

MGM in the Thirties, it was hard to imagine how they could have been considered threatening to their country.

Certainly some of the nonpolitical New York writers I'd known had been exasperated by the smugness and militancy of the Left of the Thirties. And outsiders had been alienated by the tendency of Communists to regard socialists and adherents of the New Deal as enemies because their reforms would obstruct the birth of a classless society. When I learned that many leftists of the past had been sure of their moral superiority, it seemed to me that steaming arrogance—along with their aptitude for invective—might have kindled their contemporaries' anti-Communism almost as much as the tyranny of Stalin. Often their detractors remembered scathing lectures in a living room, or charges of "political illiteracy" around a punch bowl, with a loathing that lasted for a lifetime. But the sense of superiority and the verbal assaults had disappeared by the time I visited Frognal. And the New York writers I knew had never thought the radicals dangerous.

Still, genuine liberals of the Thirties had had a further cause for aggravation: after finding themselves outmaneuvered in such organizations as the Screen Writers Guild, they had been called "social fascists" by individuals who later said that accounts of purges in the Soviet Union were falsifications by a conservative media. The literary critic Malcolm Cowley, who wasn't a Communist, wrote that the Hearst press "had told so many lies about Russia in the past that we didn't believe it when it told the truth."

Naturally those who abhorred Hitler were contemptuous of the Communists' defense of the Nazi-Soviet pact and disgusted by the rapid switches of the Party line right after the Germans invaded Russia. Liberals and leftists could share a hatred of fascism and an allegiance to the social programs of the Depression, and liberals muted their aversion to Stalin while he was our ally during World War II. Along the way, writers like Edmund Wilson had simply (although severely) disagreed with the Communists while repudiating the cold warriors' view that those who held "nonconformist political opinions" deserved the retributions of the Fifties. To Wilson our loyalty investigations seemed like a crude parody of Stalinism, and in 1956 he wrote, "Our recent security purges and political heresy-hunts must have been partially inspired by the Russian trials."

Not all American left-wingers had revered the Soviet Union; during the Depression some had been more concerned with poverty at home and fascism abroad than with the Soviet myth. Still, Communists didn't criticize the Soviets as some independent radicals did. And non-Communists could never forget the horrific immensities of Stalin's dictatorship, the murders of millions—which some of the Left did not face until the Khrushchev revelations of 1956. Conservatives and reactionaries had been right about Stalin, and others' compassion for the blacklistees was separate from an awareness of all the blood shed in the Soviet Union.

Most of the people I'd seen on those Sundays had died before the late Nineties, when recently opened Comintern archives exposed contacts between American Communist leaders and the Soviet intelligence agencies, revealed that the Americans received funds from Moscow (not quite news), that some confidential State Department correspondence was stolen in Washington and given to the Comintern. Much of the newly released archival material was fragmentary. Other Soviet documents—as well as FBI files—had already shown that the Manhattan Project was penetrated by spies; among them, the German Communist and nuclear physicist Klaus Fuchs provided vital information.

Decoded cables between Moscow and New York confirmed that Julius Rosenberg was the head of a network that passed on national defense research—about radar or types of aircraft—obtained from war plants in 1944 and 1945. He was also involved with intelligence gathering about the Manhattan Project, though perhaps not extensively. The documents make it plain that Ethel

Rosenberg was not a spy—and that the FBI knew that well before she was electrocuted.

The Frognal guests would have been shocked by those disclosures, since most Party members and leftists in general had been kept ignorant about espionage. The ex-Communists I later talked with had not believed that the Party contained spies—because it seemed so improbable that the Soviets would employ individuals already under surveillance by the FBI. Yet that is what the Soviets did. But throughout our turbulent history, my interest was and is in the American Left per se rather than those who befouled it. I'm quite sure that I met no spies; the FBI suspected Ella of being one, but lengthy efforts by the bureau produced no evidence against her.

At Frognal the excesses of the California Right were recalled with laughter as well as revulsion. In the Thirties the actor Victor McLaglen had organized a brigade of uniformed horsemen who paraded in military fashion, promising to rid Hollywood of subversives. The Light Horse Cavalry Troop, as it was called, was determined to "save America." William Randolph Hearst prevailed on Gary Cooper to be the co-founder of a similar group, the Hollywood Hussars, and George Brent headed the California Esquadrille. Schooled by army officers, these vigilantes offered their services to local authorities. But their posturings had been greeted with no more gravity than Robert Taylor's proposal, soon after the 1947 hearings, that members of the Beverly Hills Tennis Club be required to sign a loyalty oath.

Yet amid all the levity at Frognal, some were still pasting themselves together. Quite a few of the exiles had been savaged by their intimates, before the Committee or in private, and time was needed to mend the dignity which had been mutilated. Over the years I heard them say that when they were younger, most had been animated by hating Hitler rather than by revering Stalin, and that the distinction wasn't understood (or was deliberately distorted) after the war. Yet the crimes of Stalin had been hung around their necks—and astounding as that was to them, it was an extremely painful weight to bear.

The exiles' legal position was misunderstood by many Americans. Some liberals thought the blacklistees ought to have stayed at home to battle against the expansion of the domestic Cold War—disregarding the fact that most of them simply could not earn a living in the United States. Their critics also felt that people who were or had been Communists should have said so on the witness stand. But many observers didn't realize that those who admitted they'd belonged to the Party would then have to give the names of other Communists or go to prison for contempt: there was no other option. If someone conceded membership, he then lost the legal right to remain silent and would be asked to inform on others, a role that was unacceptable to anyone who came to tea at Frognal. Many informers were ex-Communists who would have been fired if they had not named others; they kept their jobs only by causing some colleagues to lose theirs.

Throughout the Fifties those who were called before an investigating committee were likely to remember the prosecution of the Hollywood Ten in 1947; numerous lawyers believed that it raised the largest questions about civil liberties of any case of that era. When the witnesses—seven screenwriters, two directors, and one writer-producer, all past or current Communists—were asked by the Committee if they were or ever had been Party members, they at first avoided answering by lambasting the Committee. At their trial for contempt of Congress, they took the First Amendment. One of the Ten, the writer Albert Maltz, told me that by doing so they aimed to make a political statement: declaring that the First Amendment forbade Congress to pass any law that could curtail the freedom of speech or opinion, that the government had no right to investigate a citizen's beliefs or associations. (In that interpretation, the First guarantees the right to remain silent as well as the right to speak.) By contesting the power of the Committee to legislate in the field of political associations, the Ten had hoped to destroy it in the courts and to rid the country of political inquisitions. Some of the Ten also invoked the entire Bill of Rights.

Lawyers who had radical clients constantly discussed the choice between the First and the Fifth Amendments. The First was considered preferable because it challenged the legality of the existence of the Committee and defended the tradition of free speech. The Fifth—which affirmed that no one could be "compelled in any criminal case to be a witness against himself"—merely shielded the individual against self-incrimination. Many Communists and ex-Communists were proud of their political past and did not want their anti-fascist or pro-union activities to be classified as "criminal." But the Hollywood Ten lost their case. Their experience showed that taking the First usually resulted in a jail sentence for contempt or in years of crippling legal costs; lawyers often warned that you needed to be rich to plead the First Amendment. The Fifth did keep many out of prison—although they were dismissed from their jobs because the Committee had deprived the Fifth of its legitimacy, and most Americans assumed that anyone who took the Fifth was a Communist. The consequences of taking the First *or* the Fifth were mentioned rather ruefully at Frognal.

Passport renewals were denied to exiles who had been uncooperative witnesses and to those who had left-wing "associations"—even if they had not been summoned by the Committee. Some passports were revoked while their owners were overseas. Starting in 1951 leftists could not obtain passports because the State Department claimed that their "conduct abroad is likely to be contrary to the best interests of the United States." It was expected that such radicals as Paul Robeson would "engage in activities which [would] advance the Communist movement" if they went to Europe. (In Robeson's case, the State Department had acted to prevent him from speaking about American racism in other countries.) Ruth Shipley, the Director of the Passport Office in the early Fifties, indicated that people who had criticized our foreign policy would not be permitted to travel. Linus Pauling, who'd opposed nuclear testing, was refused a passport to participate in a scientists' conference in London in 1952; he was refused again when Nehru invited him to India in 1954, even though the Soviets had attacked his work as "vicious" and "hostile to the Marxist view." And under the 1952 McCarran-Walter Immigration Act, foreign "undesirables" such as Pablo Picasso, Yves Montand, and Graham Greene were not allowed to enter the United States. In the meantime most of the exiles I knew could not leave England because other countries would not have let them enter or would have deported them.

At least England did not eject them. But when the blacklisted screenwriters arrived there, the British studios—then dominated by American interests—were wary of them. If their names were on the credits, their pictures couldn't be shown in the United States because the American Legion and kindred groups would picket those movies—hence American distributors wouldn't handle them. The power of the Legion was colossal: in the early Fifties, when Hollywood was already losing much of its audience to television, the producers feared that the Legion's pickets could ruin the entire movie business: millions would shun the films they condemned because it would be un-American to cross that picket line. Studio officials promised the Legion not to hire anyone who took the Fifth Amendment and they asked the Legion for its own files on suspects. The producers were afraid to retain anyone of whom the Legionnaires disapproved.

The Legion's influence extended all the way to England, where the Ealing Studios had at first seemed eager to commission DOS to write comedies; then they recoiled from his political history. Yet some of the American movie executives based in London admired those who had defied the Committee and wanted to employ them. Gradually the blacklisted began to work in Britain under pseudonyms. But writing anonymously meant they could not rely on their previous credits: it was as though they were starting their careers anew each time. As a result some earned about 15 to 20 percent of their former fees.

Some of the Frognal guests had substantial savings from the days before the blacklist, but quite a few exiles were economic refugees: they were in London because they couldn't possibly support their families at home. And all of them chafed at their anonymity. DOS wrote as Gilbert Holland, using the first and middle names of his dead brother. (Others chose pseudonyms that were all too penetrable: some wouldn't relinquish their own initials.) Larry Adler's name was expunged from the American prints of the British comedy *Genevieve,* for which he wrote the music; the credit went to the conductor Muir Mathieson. Hy Kraft couldn't have a credit for the movie of his musical *Top Banana.* When Joseph Losey and Carl Foreman made films under fictitious names, they collaborated with blacklistees whenever possible. Foreman, who wrote parts of *The Bridge on the River Kwai,* saw the Oscar for the script given to the French novelist Pierre Boulle—who could not then read or write English. So there was elation among the exiles when *Marty,* featuring the blacklisted actress Betsy Blair, and *Rififi,* made in France by blacklistee Jules Dassin, won prizes at the Cannes Film Festival.

At home there was ample gossip about the authorship of certain screenplays. Many scripts were ascribed to Dalton Trumbo of the Hollywood Ten, who worked steadily under a host of names. Ring Lardner, Jr., another of the Ten, later wrote, "To the frustration of the actual writers, some of the best work in Hollywood was being assigned by rumor to Trumbo, and the more outstanding the picture, the broader the leer with which he declined to comment." He did write *Roman Holiday,* Audrey

Hepburn's first movie, also *Gun Crazy*. Some of the other black-listees who couldn't use their names were Michael Wilson (who wrote *Friendly Persuasion* and parts of *The Bridge on the River Kwai*), Albert Maltz (co-writer of *The Robe*), Abraham Polonsky (*Odds Against Tomorrow*), Hugo Butler (Buñuel's *Adventures of Robinson Crusoe*), John Howard Lawson (co-writer of *Cry, the Beloved Country*), and Bernard Gordon (*Hellcats of the Navy,* the only movie in which both Ronald and Nancy Reagan appeared).

Books by the blacklisted were plucked out of American libraries and the State Department ordered their work removed from United States Information Agency libraries in Europe—along with Thoreau's *Walden,* which was deemed "downright socialistic." Their prose couldn't be adapted for film or radio or television: all their earlier writing was banned as well as their latest efforts. Meanwhile Hannah Weinstein, a New Yorker who produced the British television series *The Adventures of Robin Hood,* hired more than twenty blacklisted writers, including Lardner, Ian Mclellan Hunter, and Waldo Salt. The serial boomed away on the TV set at Frognal; against its surging theme song—"Feared by the bad / Loved by the good / Robin Hood / Robin Hood / Robin Hood"—the exiles spoke of dead or distant figures like Tom Mooney (framed on a bombing charge and imprisoned in California from 1916 to 1939) and labor leader Harry Bridges. The violence at Peekskill, New York, in 1949—when over a hundred people were injured by stones hurled by Legionnaires after Paul Robeson gave a concert and some policemen joined the assailants—was often mentioned by those who worked namelessly in London. All this history was new to me: how strange that I had to learn it abroad. About twenty years passed before it was publicly discussed in my own country.

At Frognal I also heard about Upton Sinclair's EPIC campaign of 1934, when the novelist won the Democratic nomination for governor after he vowed to "End Poverty in California." Because he had written an exposé of the movie business and planned to impose special taxes on the studios, the alarmed executives backed the Republican candidate, Frank Merriam, and the film industry rapidly united with *The Los Angeles Times* to portray Sinclair as a Bolshevik menace. At MGM—where DOS was co-writing *Marie Antoinette* for Norma Shearer and Tyrone Power—everyone who earned more than a hundred dollars a week was told to donate a day's wages to Merriam's campaign. MGM also produced three sham newsreels in which sinister men with beards and foreign accents championed Sinclair's candidacy, as did vagrants who were supposedly heading for California to enjoy the welfare that Sinclair would dispense. It was said that EPIC would ignite a local revolution. The "documentaries," given free to movie houses throughout the state, were originated by Irving Thalberg: this was reputed to be his only political act since his adolescence, when he'd made street-corner speeches for the Socialist Party in Brooklyn. Other studios concocted similar footage. When Sinclair lost the election, *The New York Times* reported that "political leaders attribute Sinclair's defeat to the splendid work on the part of the screen."

Frognal was a warehouse for the American past: memories of DOS's dead friends, such as Robert Benchley and Scott Fitzgerald, stayed fresh around the lunch table, and Ella recounted how Whittaker Chambers—whom she'd met while she was married to Lincoln Steffens—had asked her to take some papers from the Washington desk of her old friend William Bullitt, the first ambassador to the Soviet Union. (She wouldn't comply, but she told me Chambers had nettled her: "He gave me the feeling that if I couldn't do that, then I wasn't much good. And I didn't *want* him to think I wasn't much good!" She swore that she and Steffens had known nothing about Chambers's underground activities.) And Ella kept reminding others that DOS had helped the young Hemingway to find a New York publisher. Legendary one-liners were also preserved at Frognal. After a famous lesbian murderer of the Twenties sent her victim's uterus in a suitcase to

her new lover, Dorothy Parker was asked to define the carrier
which contained such an object. She decided that it was a snatch-
all. Her opinion of Lawrence Stallings, the co-author of *What
Price Glory?* who had tried to break up the Screen Writers Guild,
was quoted: "I wouldn't like him if he had no legs." (He had one.)

During five years of Sundays at Frognal, I came to feel that
the strength of the Left was probably more familial than religious. Outsiders who compared the American radical movement
to a church had, I think, misunderstood the power of the ties
among those who had relished working together, even though
they often fought each other. Hymns to "fraternity" would have
embarrassed them. But after at least two decades, these people
did behave like relatives; bound by affection and exasperation
throughout their common history, they appeared to be at home
with one another. And although radicals of the Thirties had often
been depicted as unsmiling drudges toiling grimly to create a socialist paradise, neither their adversaries nor the Marxist historians had acknowledged that American leftists could enjoy one
another's company. Academics of the Left and pundits of the
Right might have been disoriented by the waves of laughter rising from the garden or in the living room at Frognal, which I
quite often heard even when I was standing outside the front
door.

In his last decade Donald Ogden Stewart called himself the luck-
iest and happiest of men—and on his best days there was a gaiety
that was contagious. The style was faintly self-deprecating: he
invited you to join him in mocking himself. Hemingway caught
some of that essence in *The Sun Also Rises,* where DOS appeared
as Bill Gorton, the successful writer who longed to buy stuffed
dogs when he was drunk. (Gorton was also partially based on Bill
Smith, Hemingway's boyhood friend and fishing companion.)

With Hemingway DOS had run with the bulls during the fiesta in Pamplona in 1924—he was soon tossed and cracked a rib or two—and he later vouched for the accuracy of the novelist's account of their disastrous week in Spain in 1925. But DOS still had fond memories of the first "male festival" in Pamplona and he told me he would like to see another bull fight before he died bull fight—if only he could find the right bull.

Mild but persistent raspberries were a mark of his affection. He was proud of his lethal martinis; when I asked for a glass of wine instead, he said, "I suppose you'd order scrambled eggs at Tiffany's!" (When he was a guest, he usually behaved like a host: at others' parties he would take someone's half-empty glass, murmuring politely, "May I deal with this?" Then he would drink it.) In his seventies he was told by a stern young doctor that he must have prostate surgery, adding, "We'll operate through the penis, of course." DOS replied, "Mine or yours?"

When I first knew him in the mid-Fifties, he was still angry at his government, at being excluded from his profession, at being treated like a traitor—a formidable bitterness tinged the sweetness of his manner. I thought him a partial depressive, as many satirists are. Years after his death I was reminded of him when I read a letter Chekhov wrote to his wife, the actress Olga Knipper, during rehearsals of *The Three Sisters,* warning her not to look sad in her role: "Angry, yes, but not sad. People who have long carried a grief within them and grown used to it merely whistle a bit and brood a lot." Yet as DOS aged he insisted on his felicity: "My story is about a kid from Columbus, Ohio, who has the American dream dumped into his lap, who has it all come true. He has the Whitneys, the Vanderbilts, the Racquet Club, big salaries, success on the stage—and that guy becomes a Marxist. Give a man in America everything, and he'll turn out to fight for socialism. Now I think that's a happy story."

Once I asked him how his politics had evolved. Ella kept rushing in and disrupting his recollections, but over a series of lunches and teas I heard other parts of the story. And he was pleased when I said I wanted to tape him. Born in 1894, the son of a Republican judge, DOS was taught that "Work was a thing called success. It was connected with society and belonging to the right clubs." Moreover, "Society *was* security. And security was somehow connected with knowing the Whitneys and the Vanderbilts," although it was acceptable to know an occasional outsider, such as what Columbus called "a darn nice Jew." When he was about to graduate from Exeter and was on his way to Yale, his family lost most of its modest income, and he waited on tables, dug holes for telephone poles, and sold corsages before college proms: "I would knock on doors and hope to Christ no one was in." Before discovering that he wanted to write, he imagined himself as "the cultured vice president of a bank: I learned the first and second movements of various symphonies." Nonetheless he had an early sense of social obligation, which he felt he'd inherited from his grandfather, the first president of Fisk University, founded after the Civil War to educated freed slaves.

In the Navy during World War I—he had never been on a ship or touched a gun—he taught classes in seamanship and gunnery, where he learned how to make his students laugh at his attempts to tie a bowline. In 1921, fired from the bond business when he was broke and had to support his widowed mother, he began writing parodies for *Vanity Fair* at the suggestion of Edmund Wilson—"And the kid was off. Honestly, toots, it was as lucky as that." Planning to be the Mark Twain of his generation, he also wanted to be the life of the party—"It was a profession in those days"—and he was. Later he would be stimulated by Voltaire and Swift. But he wasn't yet political; when Robert Benchley went to Boston to testify against the judge in the Sacco and Vanzetti case, or when Dorothy Parker and Edna St. Vincent Millay picketed the statehouse, he did not accompany them: "That was none of my business."

Yet in the early Twenties he'd experienced an indignation that was common among his contemporaries; he'd believed in the war: "I really wanted to go over the top, really believed that America was fighting for a better world. Then suddenly we had Warren G. Harding and the First National Bank and the return to normalcy: *normalcy* was the word that made us angry. We were angry that we'd gone to war and it hadn't worked—the idealism with which we went to war was later betrayed. The outcome of the war was meant to be a peaceful and just society. But that wasn't what Warren G. Harding was elected for!"

In that mood he wrote *Aunt Polly's Story of Mankind*—"A very bitter book: I thought it was the *Candide* of 1923. Everybody was doing outlines of history then: Hank Van Loon and others as well as H. G. Wells. Mine had a self-satisfied pompous woman telling her young nephews and nieces how the amoeba developed into a monkey and then into a man, and then came Uncle Frederick, the vice president of the First National Bank. And that's the wonderful story of how the world is getting better, that was progress. I was angry at the Uncle Fredericks of this world: the lying hypocrites who might make another war."

During his first marriage he had "ten marvelous years of fun and dancing and Hollywood and plays and success." Two of his comedies did well on Broadway. Between 1930 and 1949 he worked on some twenty-eight movies, including *Laughter*, *Tarnished Lady*, *Smilin' Through*, *Going Hollywood*, *The Barretts of Wimpole Street*, *Kitty Foyle*, *That Uncertain Feeling*, *A Woman's Face*, *Edward, My Son*, and the screen versions of Philip Barry's *Holiday*, *The Philadelphia Story*, and *Without Love*. Like most major screenwriters in the Thirties, he had collaborators because producers thought two writers would be more productive than one, and he usually adapted plays or novels. But he was known for elegant dialogue and often he wrote the final shooting script itself.

Early on, pleasure seemed limitless. I asked what his definition of freedom had been then. He answered, "Freedom was

knowing the right person to get into a speakeasy. But there were
a few things you weren't allowed to do. You couldn't spit in certain places. And you couldn't sit in reserved seats." But almost
everything he wanted seemed attainable: "If you start on your
ass, there's no place to go but off it. I very bravely accepted happiness. I never fought it."

In 1933, when Louis B. Mayer tearfully asked him to take a
pay cut because the movie business had been devastated by the
Depression, DOS agreed to a 50 percent reduction of his salary.
At first he thought Mayer was crying about the plight of the nation, but soon he realized that the tears were for MGM. (Mayer
was an easy weeper, especially when he planned to manipulate
others.) Since DOS earned more than almost any writer in Hollywood, he didn't then see the need for protection against cuts that
the new Screen Writers Guild sought to ensure, nor did he perceive the importance of the Guild in safeguarding the salaries of
those who were paid far less than he.

In 1935 DOS was writing a play called *Insurance* in which a
wealthy man became a Communist, "But I had no idea what
Communists were like." He told me he'd consulted the doorman
of Claridge's Hotel while he was visiting London, and the man
sent him to a bookstore that recommended John Strachey's *The
Coming Struggle for Power*. During the same trip he bought
twenty-four dress shirts: twelve of them were stiff-bosomed and
the rest were soft.

The Strachey book had an enormous impact: he felt it committed him to Marxism and to the Soviet Union. He also read
André Malraux's *Man's Fate* and *The New Masses,* a periodical
unfamiliar to him. The contradictions between the bread lines
and his own life were inescapable. Having been quite poor when
young, having sported with the rich, DOS was shaken by the
Marxist view that the rich were corrupt due to the position of
their class: however decently some might behave, they were inevitably the exploiters of working people. And since his pay-

checks put him in that category, he didn't want to be identified with evil. He wrote in his memoirs, "It suddenly came over me that I was on the wrong side." If a "class war" was underway, "I had somehow got into the enemy's army." Years later he would comment on his ignorance about the Soviet Union—with no regrets for anything he did on behalf of his new convictions.

While outsiders joked about the dawning social consciousness of screenwriters who were prospering as they never had before, many in Hollywood were sincere in feeling that they owed something to the destitute while malnutrition was ravaging the country. I don't think they felt guilty for earning well. But some didn't feel entitled to hang on to all that money. It seemed imperative to donate time as well as dollars to the homeless and the hungry. The sight of people dwelling in vacant lots or eating garbage quickened a reflex of concern. And middle-class radicals of the Thirties could gain self-respect from activism.

Watching hunger marchers being clubbed by policemen in Manhattan's Union Square, learning that the Bonus Army of 1932 had been driven out of Washington by armed troops who burned the flimsy shacks where jobless veterans had camped while petitioning Congress for their bonuses, hearing about ten persons who were killed in Chicago when police fired into a crowd which was picketing Republic Steel for the right to unionize, many Americans' sense of helplessness about the Depression coexisted with a belief that something could and would be done about it. The dread of unending poverty fueled a confidence in impending change, and many thought life would improve— because it had to. Despite the economic anguish (in part, because of it) the decade was also tinged with hope: that the worst inequities would not remain unaltered.

Forty years after the British novelist and critic Philip Toynbee had left the Communist Party, he told a lecture audience that he "had always wanted to be a great writer and a good man." The latter meant "being a good Communist," and "to be a good

Communist—dutiful, hard-working, loyal, and obedient—was to be a good man." (Since the witty Toynbee was also an uproarious drunk, his friends had not discerned the lust for virtue.) Naturally the goal of goodness could breed arrogance: the loftiness of the Left which irked outsiders. But some nascent American radicals found that their endeavors gave them a sense of worth. And DOS—who wrote that he'd "wanted to be well-liked by everyone"—was on better terms with himself after an immersion in the radical movement.

For him it was insufficient to write a check for the migrant workers on strike in the Salinas Valley. In 1936 he was one of the founders of the Hollywood Anti-Nazi League and became its first president. He was also president of the League of American Writers, created by the Communist Party. Both leagues attracted many liberals and radicals as well as Communists. As DOS described those years to me, he added, "And the thing is, toots, I still have those dress shirts, because people stopped asking me to parties. I've got the shirts upstairs, they're very yellow now."

At the Conference of Western Writers in San Francisco he heard Ella Winter give a lecture. He had expected Lincoln Steffens's widow to be "a little old lady in purple and lace, and then out comes Aimée Semple McPherson! She talked politics, but it was sex, sex, sex all the way." (Ella told me that when she was a student, she never kissed anyone: "I was an intellectual and you just didn't. Kissing led to prostitution and marriage.") She and DOS met in 1936 and were married in 1939.

From 1933 onward, thousands of European Jews settled in and near Los Angeles, so the Hollywood Left was on the front line for news about the killings of Jews abroad, well before most Americans knew about them. Hollywood radicals also received information from Otto Katz—sometimes known as Rudolph Breda—a Communist leader of the German underground. Katz helped to start the Anti-Nazi League when he visited Hollywood and distributed copies of *The Brown Book of the Hitler Terror,* and he was a model for the anti-fascist in Lillian Hellman's *Watch on the Rhine*. Throughout the Thirties, DOS gave abundant energies to the League, raising money for refugees from Spain as well as Germany, organizing committees and meetings, sponsoring delegations, making speeches about the responsibility of Americans to combat fascism and to aid its victims. In the mid-Thirties, a time of isolationist fervors, not many Americans seemed to feel that what happened in Europe had any significance in the United States.

DOS was also very active in the Screen Writers Guild. Supporting civil liberties groups and labor militants, he lost some friends and he lost a cordial relationship with his employer Irving Thalberg, who wanted him to withdraw from politics long before Hollywood was investigated. (Among the producers, Thalberg was the most fiercely opposed to the Guild, and he once threatened to shut down MGM if the writers persisted in trying to form a union.) But nothing diminished DOS's efforts to increase the public's awareness of the atrocities abroad and injustice at home. There were many Nazi sympathizers in Los Angeles, where the German-American Bund kept handing out anti-Semitic leaflets. Like most on the Left, DOS felt the United States was nurturing its own brand of fascism, disguised as patriotism—the theme of his script for *Keeper of the Flame,* released in 1942.

At first the Hollywood producers backed the Anti-Nazi League "because most of them were Jewish. Then they got worried about Communists." While granting that he'd been "a romantic Marxist," DOS never told me if he had belonged to the Communist Party. (Nor did I ask: a child of the Fifties hated to do that.) But I eventually deduced that he'd been a member from about 1936 until April 1941—because he would not deny membership before that date when he sought to regain his passport in 1956. He had left the League of American Writers when that organization defended the Nazi-Soviet pact and urged the United

States to stay out of World War II. A couple of his letters to Ella (reproduced in his FBI file) show that he'd become critical of the Soviet Union, and he no longer saw Russia as "a Magic Helper." While the pact had given him great pain, it had not destroyed his belief in socialism, and he wept "with relief" when Hitler invaded the Soviet Union, grateful that the forces of anti-fascism could be reunited.

Until the hearings of 1947, which led to the jailing of the Hollywood Ten, the Hollywood Left presumed that it could withstand its opponents. DOS may not have guessed that his FBI file, begun in 1936, would one day be 915 pages long. It included Ella's file, which was started in 1927 and contained copies of some of her letters to Lincoln Steffens. Once she and DOS were married their own correspondence was monitored. The bureau faithfully listed Ella's pre-war articles for *The New York Times Magazine* ("The Soviet Way with the Child," "Our Engineers Find Romance in Russia"), and kept track of DOS's affiliations, among them the Joint Anti-Fascist Refugee Committee, the Greenwich Village Salute to the Red Army, the Friends of the Abraham Lincoln Brigade, the American Committee for Spanish Freedom, and the American Council for Democratic Greece.

DOS and Ella were on the Security Index, candidates for "custodial detention." The Internal Security Act of 1950 (also known as the McCarran Act) entitled the Attorney General to order that "dangerous or potentially dangerous" Americans be rounded up and imprisoned without a trial during "internal security emergencies" or if the country became "involved in war." Some FBI memoranda indicate that both—especially Ella—were seen as potential spies for the Soviet Union. As she sailed for Russia in wartime, an agent "examined" her luggage for "possible espionage material with negative results." The bureau began to watch them on a daily basis before she left.

Agents copied Ella's engagement book ("Dinner Hacketts,

*People's World* party at Laura Perelman's"). They also noted when
the lights in the Stewart home were turned off at night, when
DOS walked his dog ("a brown and white setter"), that he sometimes called his wife Fidget or Muffet and referred to the
Communist Party as the Railroad or the R.R., and that the couple went to see Alfred Hitchcock's *Lifeboat*. By then they realized that they were under surveillance.

DOS was blacklisted in 1950. MGM had ordered him to
"clear" himself, to say he regretted having been "duped" and to
give names. He refused—"I was terribly proud of everything I'd
done"—and his contract was cancelled. He and Ella moved to
England, where the American embassy in London kept the FBI
abreast of their activities, and DOS wrote English dialogue for
Roberto Rossellini's *Europa '51,* additional dialogue for Lewis
Milestone's *Melba,* and the script for *Escapade*; his name could
not appear on any of them. With Joseph Losey he wrote a screenplay of Strindberg's *The Father,* but it wasn't produced. His passport was revoked in 1952, so he couldn't go to Germany to see a
production of his play *The Kidders*, nor to Venice to finish his
draft of the shooting script of David Lean's *Summertime,* which
another writer completed. And so he both festered and flourished
in Hampstead, digesting his disgust with the recent past while
savoring the rewards of the earlier years, and welcoming those
who remembered them.

The genial anarchy of Frognal sprang primarily from the temperament of Ella, who had been born in Australia and raised in
England. When she could pause in an orbit that seemed to demand her presence in sixteen places at once, it was engrossing to
hear her reminisce about her Fabian youth at the London School
of Economics or about Lincoln Steffens, who seemed like a resi-
dent of the household—not a ghost, but a part of the ménage.

Sometimes I felt he had left Frognal for only an hour or so, as if he were out conducting a seminar or taking a stroll.

Steffens wrote in his *Autobiography* that when he first met Ella—a twenty-one-year-old employed by Felix Frankfurter at the Versailles Conference—"It seemed to me that she was one of the happiest things I had ever seen" as he watched her "dancing about among the delegates, lobbyists, and correspondents." (For those who knew her decades later, when she was periodically stricken with clinical depressions, there was a poignancy in that description.) But Steffens recalled her as "joyous. . . . This girl danced. Her eyes danced, her mind, her hands, her feet danced as she ran—she literally trotted about on her errands." She was thirty-two years his junior, and Steffens was "fascinated by this personification of the younger generation." He soon became the tutor of the "young genius." "Forced . . . to clear my own mind while I was clearing hers," eager to "disillusion" her of liberal ideas and to endow her with more radical "illusions," to saturate her in "the facts" he thought she neglected, he chided her for "excessive quickness" and "impatience" and was proud of her development under his aegis.

But some years after he embarked on Ella's education, he felt she had enriched his own: that she had revealed America to him when she saw it for the first time. Indeed some historians concluded that in the long run she influenced him—particularly in furthering his enthusiasm for the Soviet Union after she went there in 1930 and 1931, although his perspective remained more sophisticated than hers. (Max Eastman, after he'd renounced the Left, claimed that Ella—"unmellowed by experience" and "born to be a zealot"—had converted Steffens "from a sentimental rebel . . . to a hard-cut propagandist of the party line.") Bruce Bliven of *The New Republic* credited Ella with "bullying" Steffens into writing his autobiography. Bliven wrote, "It had to be snatched from him almost page by page and rushed to the publisher, to keep him from destroying the manuscript."

In Steffens's final years, as Ella lectured and wrote about
Russia, organized support for the migrant lettuce, cherry, and
cotton pickers in California, covered the great 1934 waterfront
strike in San Francisco for *The New Masses*, and headed the John
Reed Club in Carmel, the couple was a target of American
Legionnaires. After a local paper stated that Ella had had sex
with twenty-nine black men, Steffens said, "Why not thirty?"

Although some of her declarations sounded simple, she left a
trail of complexities behind her: you could puzzle over one of her
pronouncements for days. While she never acquired the reflective intellect that Steffens envisioned, ardor propelled her
through the anti-nuclear protests that began in England in the
Fifties. As an activist she seemed almost capable of cloning herself—you might meet her on the stairs and then suddenly sight
her in the garden—and she gleefully recalled how she and the
film distributor Thomas Brandon used to infiltrate German-
American Bund rallies during the Thirties to shout anti-fascist
slogans from opposite sides of the hall, so that the audience would
assume that dozens were present: "They would call out, 'They're
here!' 'No, they're there!' and they never knew that there were
only two of us!" Activism could also make her inaccessible: in
Hollywood, when DOS asked his MGM secretary to phone her
and the line was busy for hours, he finally said, "Oh hell, get me
my first wife!" Sometimes I received postcards from her with
nothing written on them: the invitation or the command had
been forgotten after the card was hastily addressed.

Amid the constant drama of distraught au pairs—the young
women quit Frognal because they couldn't possibly keep pace
with Ella—the past and present could be scrambled: in the late
Seventies, when I told her that *The Los Angeles Times* had improved, she cried, "I *spit* on *The L.A. Times*!"—because of its anti-
union policies of 1910. Change, for which she had labored, could
be overlooked: wicked institutions or individuals were not expected to redeem themselves. Yet she had no respect for bound-

aries, nor could she be deterred in any quest: in pursuit of some elusive information, she told me to ring a film historian she'd known; I objected that he was dead. Ella barked, "Then call someone who isn't!"

I heard her say that the Hollywood Left had made many errors, especially in their misunderstanding of the Soviet Union: "Some of what we believed wasn't true. But that doesn't matter, because we *worked* for what we believed in." Functioning rather like a cyclone, she could be criticized for rashness, for inaccuracy, for running off the road, but not for indecision—while others pondered, she hurtled forward, as unjudging as a dynamo.

Somewhat surprised by the rebirth of feminism, she—although an early suffragist—had been persuaded by her Fabian friends that inequality was a social condition unrelated to gender and that socialism would give women the same rights as men. But she had always led an unrestricted life. Frognal used to razz her because her small son had had to stand waiting for her outside men's rooms because she rarely bothered to read the signs on public toilets. Yet she did acknowledge a few differences between the sexes. The novelist Ira Wolfert said Ella thought men were created to run errands and carry heavy objects, and he was one of many she encumbered with large items to lug through customs.

Alternating with her depressions, there were manic periods when her instincts seemed frantic beyond focus. Then she would whirl into pressuring a Member of Parliament to raise questions in the House of Commons about a licorice candy called Nigger Babies, or berating the young Italian maid for not wearing socks while serving meals, or trying to arrange London concerts for Paul Robeson in hopes that the State Department would be embarrassed into returning his passport (the Let Robeson Sing committee did achieve a concert via amplified transatlantic telephone, attended by a big audience), hurling fruit rinds from the iced-tea pitcher over the garden wall until the neighbors' solicitor arrived to remonstrate, organizing a children's party, ringing up a new acquaintance who was said to be ironic and witty: "Why aren't you ironic and witty with *me?*," scrubbing her rubber plant with steel wool until it collapsed with a hiss, and harassing her lemur. She found that nocturnal animal bad company because it slept in the daytime, so she banged on its cage or placed it next to a bellowing television set to keep it awake. Since it couldn't sleep at night, the rings beneath its sunken eyes grew even deeper, and it had no relief until she went away for a week; then it keeled over. On her return it fled squawking from her arms up the chimney and was not seen again. Some of us thought she should have been more sympathetic to its habits because she too was given to sudden naps—especially at the movies, where she would doze, then jerk violently awake, exclaiming "Needs some Stewart dialogue!" and then plunge into slumber again.

Sexual curiosity was still a powerful stimulant for Ella when she was over seventy: at times it took the form of recollection. As a girl she spent years trying to find out what Oscar Wilde's crime was. Since her parents provided no sex education, she thought that babies were born from the anus and she wondered how they were kept clean of shit. Her mother had told her that men were after only one thing; therefore when Steffens first touched her hand, she said, "So you're a rotter, like all the other men." Steffens dropped her hand. Much later, when she was dining with him at the Russell Hotel in Bloomsbury and was racked with menstrual cramps, he took her to his room and offered some gin. Before long the hotel manager walked in on them: Ella was in bed, the bottle of gin was nearby—"If you were Toulouse-Lautrec, you couldn't do it better," DOS reflected. The manager ordered her to leave and Ella, who was mortified, confessed that she was "unwell." The man asked how she could have been well downstairs in the dining room and unwell in the bedroom, and she was ousted after rejoining that "A woman is sometimes well *and* unwell." That tale, often repeated, was part of the lore at Frognal.

Ella could display a beguiling frankness about matters which were unflattering to her. She recalled asking Joseph Losey, "Why is it that I like you so much and you don't like me?" He replied, "Maybe that's the reason." After the Thurbers visited Frognal, they reported that "the hollow laughter began immediately." Ella said of Jim, "He thinks I'm a Thurber woman!" When she and DOS began to write their separate memoirs, his work room was directly above hers and when there was a lull in his typing, she pounded on the ceiling with a broom handle. One day he sweetly informed her that he had switched to a ballpoint pen: thereafter she wouldn't be able to know if he was writing or just checking out the cricket scores in a newspaper. Ella was infuriated; she felt his wit should be employed to wring the withers of history every day—and besides (as she often said), she couldn't make jokes herself.

Her daily life was a series of challenges: crossing a street, she would charge into heavy traffic with her head lowered and a broad-brimmed hat tilted over her eyes: brakes screamed and drivers yelled, but she wouldn't look at them. She kept redecorating her home: paint samples and scraps of rugs and curtains were scattered throughout the rooms. As one friend said, objects spoke to Ella. Chairs, tables, birdcages, chests, and lamps cried out to her: put me in the basement, throw me in the attic, paint me green, saw me in half, cut my legs off, sell me! She ruined an antique dollhouse by trying to restyle it. Acting on impulse and seizing others' property were reflexes; when my father and my husband visited Frognal on Christmas Eve, Ella asked to borrow the former's Swiss pocket knife (his favorite) and the latter's umbrella (his best), pretended to mislay them, and when I went to recover those prized possessions I found that she had wrapped both and given them away as Christmas presents. The knife, with its many blades, its corkscrew, files, and scissors had gone to an eight-year-old: impossible to take it back. The umbrella, despite a shiny metal ring engraved with the owner's name, had been mailed to someone in Canada. Both men refused to go to Frognal again.

Initially I thought her ruthless, probably destructive, even though DOS was clearly devoted to her. (After they had a lively quarrel about whether to be cremated or buried, he said, "Let's dissolve together, dear." He meant it and ultimately they did— dying less than three days apart.) Many adored him but disliked her, although a few of their intimates felt he used her as a shield, making her shoulder the unpleasant tasks or play the ogre when he wanted to evade others—so that he could continue to appear angelic while Ella was regarded as a scoundrel. At times he grace- fully undercut her: when she named a cat Kim Il Sung, he told everyone to call it Pussy. Ella often behaved outrageously, even abominably. Hence it was striking that she was well-loved: by both husbands, by some lifelong friends. One day when she made a scene at lunch and then dashed into the kitchen to browbeat the maid, DOS told the young writer Sally Belfrage what he would inscribe on Ella's tombstone: "She was awful but she was worth it."

And over the years it became plain that it was she who had made this community congeal, who made Frognal an indispen- sable refuge for émigrés and dissidents, especially those who had no passports and were locked into England. Many of them might have remained isolated—rootless or rudderless—had it not been for the energies Ella brought to reuniting them: she did realize how much they needed that coherence. The English assumed that the exiles were overjoyed to have left the repulsive country which had abused them. But few of their English acquaintances understood that these Americans missed their own culture—or that they sometimes felt like amputated limbs.

At moments the British used the blacklisted as exhibits: to prove that Britain was a great democracy. So Frognal was a haven where the exiles could escape the strains of diplomacy; as one recalled, "We could go to Frognal and say, 'This fucking coun- try! The toilets don't work—' without being insulting to the English." The commonwealth of Frognal may also have protect- ed the blacklisted from the spasms of guilt that punished persons often feel simply because they have been punished. (Elsewhere I encountered various penitents of the Thirties. But although mistakes were admitted, self-flagellation seemed scarce at Frognal.) And like many who were at first alarmed by Ella's tendency to pounce and scatter, I became fond of her and grateful for the confederacy she had created, the sanctuary she had made.

When you entered Frognal, as the heavy front door slowly swung open on its hinges, you were almost overwhelmed with objects: Picasso's sketches and Lissitzky's paintings and a magnificent Mondrian portrait of a chrysanthemum and a large wooden sphinx's head over the fireplace competed for your dazed attention: the house itself was an event. (It was also a zoo: parrots, a monkey, mynah birds, cats and dogs, all gibbering or wailing between their sporadic feedings.) Within the walls stacked with numerous Klees, Chagall drawings, and ancient African carvings, there were glass cabinets crowded with small pre-Columbian sculptures and Asante gold weights; Peruvian puppets and embroideries from Eastern Europe could distract the eye from drawings by George Grosz. As guests inspected the Marini horseman rearing up in the living room and the Jo Davidson statue in the terraced garden, they were apt to carry their teacups and ashtrays around with them, since there were few bare surfaces at Frognal. New acquisitions appeared while old ones vanished, as evidence of Ella's fiscal talents: in Hollywood she'd invested DOS's salary in works of art, and after he was blacklisted they lived comfortably by selling one painting or sculpture at a time.

Among the frequent visitors were Cedric Belfrage, editor of the *National Guardian* until he was deported; his daughter Sally Belfrage, author of *A Room in Moscow* and later, books on Mississippi and India and Northern Ireland; psychiatrist Josephine Martin; the British writer John Collier, who was particularly helpful to the blacklisted; the socialist playwright Benn Levy and the actress Constance Cummings; Eileen O'Casey and Shivaun O'Casey; the actor Sam Wanamaker; Ingrid Bergman; Kenneth Tynan and Elaine Dundy; folklorist and musicologist Alan Lomax, who occasionally brought his guitar; and Larry Adler minus his harmonica.

Bergman—expansive and unstarlike—loved to talk, and she had an engaging tendency to rush into subjects that intrigued everyone, such as the expectation that *Casablanca* would be a catastrophe. She hardly became acquainted with Bogart because he was off fighting with the producer and the director about the chaotic state of the film. Bergman said the script was in such disarray that the action was invented from day to day, and no one knew how the movie would end. She told us that two conclusions were planned: in one of them, she would have stayed with Bogart for good. But the renunciation scene was shot first and the filmmakers decided to use it. Ella said she loathed that ending.

At Frognal Larry Adler was called "the bush baby": his small triangular face with deep-set eyes looked like Ella's lemur. Adler had taken a very public stand against the Committee and had raised money for Henry Wallace's 1948 presidential campaign. Igor Cassini, the Hearst gossip columnist, had accused Adler and the tap dancer Paul Draper, who often performed together, of peddling "Red propaganda." That inspired a woman from Greenwich, Connecticut, to write letters to the press, saying that they were "pro-Communists" and that their earnings would be sent to Moscow. Adler and Draper sued her for libel. Filing the suit required them to swear in preliminary affidavits that they had never been Communists. But the attacks from columnists Walter Winchell and Westbrook Pegler (known to the Left as Pestbrook Wiggler) continued; Cassini called for their deportation, many bookings were cancelled, and Adler and Draper lost their suit. Adler settled in London, where he played Bach and Gershwin and Ravel and music from his own bar mitzvah all over the city. The State Department almost rescinded his pass-port—until it was discovered that the musician had been mis-taken for a Leonard Adler of *The Brooklyn Daily Eagle*, allegedly a Communist. Yet Larry Adler remained on the blacklist.

Abraham and Sylvia Polonsky, Harold Clurman, the lawyer Leonard Boudin, and the lyricist E. Y. Harburg checked in at Frognal whenever they passed through London. Salka Viertel, the former actress who wrote several of Garbo's movies, came from her home in Klosters, Switzerland; the Frognal gatherings were rather like sequels to her Sundays in Santa Monica, where the Hollywood Left had mingled with expatriate artists from the late Thirties until the early Fifties. Katharine Hepburn—who'd starred in four of DOS's screenplays—strode to and fro between the house and the flowerbeds for brisk bouts of weeding; equally imperious and cordial, she was critical of the condition of the gar-den tools and showed no tolerance for rust.

When Carl Foreman's *The Mouse That Roared* was being filmed in England, Jean Seberg came to tea: after the disasters of *Saint Joan* and *Bonjour Tristesse,* she seemed relieved to be in a small movie. She spoke angrily to me about her experiences with producer-director Otto Preminger, who had launched her ca-reer—which already appeared to be fading. (She had not yet been discovered by the French directors.) Working with Preminger at seventeen, she'd expected an adult to provide her with guidance, but she said he had mainly dispensed humiliation and had given her little direction in her first two films. Whenever we met at Frognal she talked about her upbringing in Marshalltown, Iowa; like me, she seemed to crave the company of other Americans. And she enjoyed shocking me by repeating that she and her high school classmates had believed that you could get pregnant from necking. Because anxiety delayed their periods, the girls thought they were pregnant almost all the time. Since my reaction amused her, I did not say that she'd told me that story before.

The Berliner Ensemble visited Frognal only a few weeks after

Brecht's death, when the group was performing in London. His widow Helene Weigel had been a friend of Ella's since the Thirties, when the Los Angeles community of German refugees included Fritz Lang and Thomas Mann, who wrote *Doctor Faustus* in Hollywood; Brecht had written *Galileo* there. Despite their immense loss, the Brecht troupe joked about the playwright's idiosyncracies. They referred to their arguments with him about props and described how Brecht had wanted a character to wear a giant ear as a symbol for spying: finally the actor had rebelled against that huge organ and battled with Brecht until it was eliminated. (In California Brecht had realized that the FBI was tapping his phone; to confuse the eavesdroppers, Weigel sometimes read recipes from a Polish cookbook over the phone to a friend who didn't know the language. Although the FBI kept Brecht under surveillance for thirteen years, the phone taps were cancelled after two.)

As such disparate persons sat in the large living room, crumbling chunks of Ella's stale fruitcake rather than trying to chew them, dodging paper gliders flung by the smallest guests, memories rose with the steam from the electric kettle. The massive Popular Front of 1935 to 1939, when liberals and radicals had collaborated to strengthen the forces of anti-fascism and unionism, had seemed to show that all sorts of Americans could perceive a kinship between international and domestic issues when democracy was at stake.

The excitement of building the guilds in Hollywood—above all the Screen Writers Guild—had been heightened by the knowledge that Los Angeles had long been a violently anti-labor town. The film industry had hated unions ever since the advent of sound had precipitated the organizing of technicians, and Hollywood's anti-Communism was closely allied to the animosity toward labor. A couple of Frognal visitors had worked for trade unions before they arrived in Hollywood, and they relished their recollections of "practical victories"—as when the National

Labor Relations Act of 1935 had legalized the right of workers to organize. (The establishment of Social Security, also in 1935, was interpreted as a sign that the country was moving to the left.) Abraham Polonsky spoke of the formation of the Congress of Industial Organizations (CIO) as a historic moment "when the practical and the prophetic come together."

Screenwriters had been on the forefront of the Hollywood Left and their union—despite all the internal fighting—was the most effective of the talent guilds. But the deterioration of the labor movement continued to sadden many of its early allies; for them it was still painful to acknowledge that some trade unions could become reactionary or corrupt, or both. But all the defeats of the postwar era could not erase the memory of what it had been like to win—when a union contract was signed, when the Nazis were vanquished.

Listening to the Left over the decades, I came to eschew the word "McCarthyism," also "the McCarthy era," terms that reduce the whole history of anti-Communism to the behavior of one person. The senator was a by-product of the period, not its creator; he merely capitalized on an already fertile movement when he needed an issue for his re-election campaign of 1952. He considered promoting the St. Lawrence Seaway or developing a new pension plan. But when a priest suggested Communism, McCarthy seized on the subject that made him famous in 1950.

Many assume that "McCarthyism" died when he lost his power in 1954. He himself was dead in 1957, but the blacklist outlived him, lasting well into the Sixties and demolishing careers for nearly two decades. And some who called him "dreadful" really meant that someone else could do a better job, that McCarthy was besmirching the cause of anti-Communism with the sleaziness of his style, his panoramic lies, and his zeal in abusing the Establishment—as when he said that General George Marshall was "always and invariably serving the world power of the Kremlin." Many of McCarthy's critics were incensed because he molested numerous non-Communists, but the civil liberties of Communists was hardly a popular issue.

Although most Americans who'd joined the Communist Party in the Thirties had resigned before 1950, the small and steadily shrinking organization was evoked by McCarthy and other demagogues as though it was enormous. McCarthy thrived for a little more than four years because of his talent for manipulating the media and because he gave the impression that Communists had *already* perverted parts of our government, and because politicians feared that he could wreck their careers by turning the voters against them. He was skilled at galvanizing hatred, particularly among those who felt they'd been disdained or ignored by Northeastern liberals. For a time he succeeeded in paralyzing Truman, and then Eisenhower, by keeping them on the defensive while he sabotaged members of their administrations. Still, he was riding a tide that had swelled before he learned how to swim in it. After 1945 many politicians had found that reviling Communists (real or imaginary) was beneficial to their careers. No doubt some believed what they were saying or came to; repetition usually stimulates conviction.

At Frognal there were disagreements about whether anyone was entitled to be surprised by the torrents of anti-Communism which had flooded the country after World War II. Some stressed that the fear of international socialism had long been intrinsic to the nation, that Americans had recoiled from it as an alien concept—especially since most Communists of the Twenties were foreign-born—and that this emotion was only temporarily muted by our wartime alliance with the Russians. As soon as the war ended, the fear grew "when you took the heel off it," Polonsky observed.

The Palmer raids of 1919 and 1920—when the young J. Edgar Hoover had arranged the sweeping arrests of some ten thousand allegedly left-wing immigrants—and the execution of Sacco and Vanzetti were cited as examples of the long-term dread of "Bolsheviks within the gates." Prior to World War I, as millions of newcomers were arriving from Europe, the nationwide repugnance toward foreigners—seen as sly, shabby people who were believed to import diseases like bubonic plague—was thought to have fueled the fear of anarchists and syndicalists and other precursors of the American Communist Party.

Since such sentiments had been rabid in the early Twenties— even after the Red Scare had abated because public figures had condemned its excesses—some at Frognal felt that the Left should not have expected to have a role in the mainstream, not even during the Depression. Long before the Cold War, Hoover had convinced much of the populace that leftists endangered the security of the whole nation. I was told that many Americans had feared Communism more than fascism: because most patriots believed that ours was the finest democracy in the world, hence fascism could never develop in the United States—whereas the New Deal seemed to threaten the country with socialism, which would turn into Communism. And the anti-labor campaign of the Right, augmented immediately after World War II, appeared almost inevitable in response to the gains that unions had made during the Roosevelt years.

But others felt that the expansion of public hostility to the Left in the late Forties had been so rapid that they couldn't have foreseen it. Their attitude had been: "We'd just fought a war against oppression—how could that happen in *our* country?" The atmosphere of "Big Three Unity" was recalled. So was General Douglas MacArthur's 1942 tribute to the Soviet Union—when he urged the Allies to "unite in salute to that great Army and that great Nation which so nobly strives with us for the victory of liberty and freedom"—and the hopes roused by the first United Nations conference in San Francisco in 1945. Laughing briefly, Polonsky said, "All politics consists of false promises and real consequences."

Other misapprehensions about the past were exhumed at Frognal. For example, the Left had at first thought the Hollywood Ten would win their case. Although the Ten knew they would be cited for contempt—for declining to confirm or deny Party membership—and that they would lose in the trial court and the appellate court, and that they risked a year in jail, they did think they would be vindicated in the Supreme Court. Their lawyers had anticipated at least a five-to-four ruling and they had moved to postpone the case until after the 1948 elections, reasoning that the Supreme Court would be affected if Henry Wallace did well—if he received five to seven million votes. (He got slightly over one million.) But the two most liberal members of the court, Frank Murphy and Wiley B. Rutledge, died in the summer of 1949, before the second round of hearings—and that changed the composition of the Court, which turned down the Ten's petition to be heard. In 1950 they all went to prison. Radicals all over the country were stunned when they were jailed.

It was also repeated that in 1947 leftists did not foresee blacklisting. They hadn't guessed that individuals on the House Committee would tell producers like Jack Warner that the studios should expel "ideological termites," and they accepted the assurance of Eric Johnston, the president of the Motion Picture Association, that there would never be a blacklist. The reasons given for not employing the undesirables were nonpolitical: actors were informed that they were too short or too tall, too old, "not the right type" for a particular role. John Randolph later told me, "Suddenly you heard that the part had been rewritten for a midget." Since they couldn't work anonymously, as writers did—Lee J. Cobb said, "It's the only face I have"—some actors lost at least fifteen years out of their professional lives.

Writers were almost as easily rejected: I heard that when Waldo Salt was fired by RKO, he was told it had nothing to do with his politics, that he just wasn't writing well. Naturally those who were notified that their talents were dwindling sometimes came to think that was true: they could no longer feel confident of their calling. An actor who knew that the studios didn't dare to cast him would wonder if, after all, he was a mediocre performer. Directors and writers grappled with work blocks and self-doubt. Albert Maltz told me he became dubious of what he produced after being blacklisted; remembering how demoralized he'd been, he drew on an image from baseball: "As pitchers say, I lost my rhythm."

At Frognal informers were lampooned as well as despised. Contempt for those who had betrayed their principles out of fear—or who apparently had no principles at all—filtered through the smoky dusk at teatime. And Frognal was intrigued by Arthur Miller's *A View from the Bridge* when it opened in London in 1958. Some saw the play as a reply to *On the Waterfront*—that impassioned defense of the informer directed by Elia Kazan and written by Budd Schulberg; both ex-Communists had been highly cooperative witnesses. In his own waterfront drama, Miller, a non-Communist who'd refused to give names to the Committee, had portrayed the informer as a disgrace to his community: the man was not presented as a villain, but his unforgivable act ruined his life. Yet when Miller expanded and reworked the play for its London production, he hoped that audiences might sympathize with the protagonist.

Long afterward Miller told me the play wasn't conceived as

an answer to Kazan's film, but that it was "an attempt to throw a different light on the whole informing theme," which he felt had been "terribly misused" in *On the Waterfront*. Still, many leftists thought the two works must be closely related, since the press reported that Miller had withdrawn his friendship from Kazan (his former director) for years after Kazan named sixteen persons.

Throughout the 1951 investigations of the movie industry, the Hollywood Left listened to the hearings on the radio every day to learn whose names were being uttered. Most informers named John Howard Lawson, the first president and founder of the Screen Writers Guild and head of the Hollywood Communist Party: it was like saying Amen at the end of a prayer. There was a good deal of rumination about the personalities of the informers. Carl Foreman told me that some who had been extra-militant—extremists who "tended to jump for the barricades when there was no need to"—became informers. Foreman thought they had once had fantasies of heroism or martyrdom, displaying "a desire to be burned at the stake *until* the fire is lit," and that an inherent volatility had enabled them to swing wildly from Left to Right.

In Hollywood "A man has to eat" was a recurrent statement from cooperative witnesses which particularly disgusted the Left; I was told it was the cliché of the era. That justification for informing came from some for whom luxuries had become necessities, when deprivation might have meant parting with the Beverly Hills mansion, the pool, the staff of servants. Protecting a lush way of life was also rationalized with "My first responsibility is to my family." Eventually there was sympathy among radicals for informers with waning careers and inadequate salaries—and certainly for those with sick children or relatives to provide for. But responsibilities that included yachting won no compassion from the blacklisted. Theirs was the traditional American scorn for the betrayal of the childhood password or the schoolyard confidence, the vows of brotherhood taken on the playground. In the ethics of Twain and Tarkington, *you don't tell*: not even if the Indians light a fire underneath you, not when the rival cowboys uncoil the rope to string you up. Polonsky remembered that Dante sent betrayers to the Ninth Circle of Hell.

At the beginning of *The Crucible* Arthur Miller had written, "Old scores could be settled on a plane of heavenly combat between Lucifer and the Lord," and that "the envy of the miserable toward the [fortunate] could and did burst out in the general revenge." In Hollywood it was believed that certain informers wanted the jobs of the best-paid writers of the Left. Dalton Trumbo earned more than any writer in the industry, whereas Martin Berkeley—who named 161 people—was usually assigned to second-rate animal pictures; his foremost credit was *My Friend Flicka*. (Ring Lardner, Jr., observed that Berkeley was unable to write dialogue for humans.) Berkeley named some of the producers' favorite writers, DOS and Trumbo among them. Hopes that the Supreme Court would rule that blacklisting was illegal were defunct by 1951, when the practice accelerated.

Since no informer was going to proclaim that his motives were sordid or that he was terrified of the Committee, many proffered an ideology to support their actions: Communism was as much of a menace at home as in Russia. Their critics replied that the informers' positions on Stalin and the Soviet Union were perfectly understandable, but some doubted their sincerity— because most had discovered that they detested Communism only when they were summoned by the Committee. As for those who claimed that the Left had ensnared and defiled them at an early age, DOS said he still believed "the Thirties were Hollywood's finest hour" and that he could never quite forgive people who disowned their past convictions and called themselves dupes.

The naming of intimates had set off shock waves because the Hollywood Left was such a family: it was as though some informers had done violence to their closest kin. (Richard Collins named Waldo Salt; Collins had been best man at Salt's first wedding.) Years later the once-blacklisted actress Betsy Blair said to me that she had not been especially disillusioned by the behavior of the informers, but that she had been thrilled by the conduct of the non-cooperators. That probably meant, she added, that everyone must harbor an expectation of corruption due to the ambitions which ignite almost any career. No one at Frognal had been unambitious. Many continued to suffer from the loss of their vocations. But when laughter rose in protest as Ella waved her large knife and threatened to cut more slices of inedible cake (DOS said she looked like Lady Macbeth) or when Bronx cheers greeted a botched pun, I sensed a special kind of loyalty among those who were entitled to mock one another—since they had sustained each other's dignity when it was assaulted from all sides.

There were warm words for Franklin Roosevelt at Frognal, particularly from DOS. Perhaps the over-assurance of the Thirties radicals—which had left them unprepared for the Cold War—was partially due to their reliance on Roosevelt: his presence in the White House had made them feel powerful when they weren't. Yet some were still objecting that he had "saved capitalism": that the seeds of socialist principles embedded in the New Deal had actually been smothered by his administration, that the compromises prevented the development of socialism. In the Fifties the conservative Peter Viereck praised the New Deal's "revolution-preventing social reforms"—thereby concurring with radicals who felt that FDR had undermined their goals.

Frognal was engrossed by the news bulletins when Bulganin and Khrushchev visited England in April 1956 and amused when the Queen invited them to tea. In those days it wasn't easy for someone of my generation to see why some American leftists still seemed to feel a linkage with what happened in Russia, even though the ties had weakened. Technically one could understand what the Soviet Union had meant to them in the Thirties, when the first socialist country in the world had been the experiment they so eagerly hoped would succeed—when so much emotion had gone into upholding the Soviet Union's right to exist. I also knew that many hoped Russia would change enormously in the Khrushchev years, hoped that repression would not recur there, and that it would at last become a socialist democracy.

So there was still an appreciation of the concept, an old tropism that hadn't expired. In the late Fifties I found this puzzling, since I was becoming acquainted with the British Left, which showed almost no interest in Russia. But later I caught a clue to some radicals' feelings when I heard an elderly American trade unionist quoted on the Soviet Union: "It's my mother. She may be a whore, she may be a thief, she may be a junkie. But she's my mother. I'm not going to throw her out or leave her on the streets . . ."

I wasn't present when Frognal discussed Khrushchev's revelations at the Twentieth Congress in detail, though I could see that DOS was tremendously upset. But I was on hand when the Russians invaded Hungary in the fall. International attention had been centered on the Suez crisis. But then the Soviet tanks rolled into Budapest, and I heard DOS express his revulsion with the Soviet Union. Now he and his guests were appalled that the new—and supposedly more enlightened—Soviet government had behaved just as murderously as its predecessor. They mentioned Stalin more than the Soviet leaders of 1956. DOS bitterly recalled the contortions that had seemed necessary to defend many of Stalin's actions, and his violations of Marxism were gloomily explored by those over fifty or sixty. DOS told me that he still believed in Marxism and that it would be fulfilled one day—though not in his lifetime.

Only a couple of voices demurred, arguing that John Foster Dulles and the CIA must be partly responsible for manipulating the rebellion of the Hungarians. (After all, Eisenhower had pledged in 1952 to "roll back" the Iron Curtain and to "liberate" the "captive peoples" of Eastern Europe. But that was campaign talk; he wouldn't have risked a major war over Hungary.) Some leftists suspected that Prime Minister Imre Nagy's appeal to the United States and Britain for aid meant that counter-revolution was possible—hence the necessity of bringing in Soviet troops. But a few others sadly replied that the CIA could have had no entrée if Moscow had not maintained a dictatorship for eleven years.

A full fifty years later, newly opened archives concerning our Radio Free Europe showed that its broadcasts led Hungarians to believe that Western governments and the United Nations would provide troops to support the revolutionaries. The documents did not indicate that outsiders had inspired the revolution—but that many Hungarians were killed because they fought while hoping for help that was never going to come.

Years afterward a former Communist told me that the exposé of Stalin's atrocities had been far more painful for her colleagues than the blacklist. Finally they knew that they had admired a regime while it was killing millions of its own citizens, that anti-fascists who had fought Hitler had also been terrorists. Some leftists remarked on Khrushchev's courage in unveiling the vileness of Stalin. But some long-term American radicals were troubled because the Soviets did not resolve the question of how Marxism and the Revolution itself could have been corrupted.

After DOS and Ella died in 1980, their New York friends assembled in a large Upper West Side apartment to honor their memory. In the midst of the tributes, Edward Albee said that they had been "betrayed by history." For the leftists of their generation that had happened not once but twice: as the monstrosities of Stalin's Russia became apparent and when their own government had called them un-American. DOS and Ella had had no taste for sacrifice; early on they had not guessed that punishments awaited them. But knowing that they had been proud of their efforts and remembering how they had survived the bleakest chapters of their lives, I hoped that the satisfactions had outweighed the tribulations.

Charlie and Oona Chaplin were often at Frognal during the filming of *A King in New York*. For the Sunday tribe, Chaplin's recent history was almost as significant as his dimensions as an artist. The lurid fallout from his 1944 paternity trial—Representative John Rankin later referred to him as "the perverted subject of great Britain who has become notorious for his forcible seduction of white girls" and urged that he be deported—the invective from right-wingers when he entreated the Allies to enter World War II long before Pearl Harbor, the pickets organized by American Legionnaires who marched outside movie theaters showing *Monsieur Verdoux* until it was withdrawn from circulation, plus the success of the Legion and the Catholic War Veterans in dissuading many theater owners and some television stations from reviving his silent films—had all climaxed in the Attorney General's decision in 1952 that Chaplin (who was en route to England for the premiere of *Limelight*) could not return to the United States without a hearing on charges of "moral turpitude and Communist sympathies." The Immigration Service was forbidden to admit him unless his "beliefs and associations" were thoroughly investigated.

Chaplin stayed away, repeating that he wasn't a Communist but "a peacemonger." When the Legion promised to picket *Limelight,* the movie was cancelled by Twentieth Century–Fox's west coast theater chains—in keeping with Rankin's recommendation that Chaplin's "loathsome pictures be kept from the eyes of Amercan youth." Other theaters cancelled too, and *Limelight* did not play in Hollywood for twenty years. The fact that the American government demanded a million dollars in back taxes from him was deemed as punishment at Frognal. Sometimes the issues seemed fused: you couldn't tell if the accusations concerning his "moral worth" or his politics or his taxes made him angriest. As an exile of several years, he seemed thoroughly out of touch with the United States. Yet although he sounded muddled, no one could fault his rage. He had been used as an example, exhibited as a warning to others, as though his work as well as his opinions should be a source of shame.

Chaplin needed a dedicated audience and it was your duty as a guest to respond as a spectator, even if only three people were present. (The critic Robert Warshow wrote that all Chaplin's performances contained "one insistent personal message": a demand to be loved, and I think that was what we were seeing at Frognal.) Clearly he craved admiration from strangers as much as from friends. Leaping to his feet to snap his fingers and warble the theme song from *A King in New York*—"Mister, won't you hurry / And get out your money / Put a nickel in the slot, I'm getting hot"—or acting out an interview he'd just given to a reporter from *Time*: "I said to that young man, you can tell them that the only thing Charlie Chaplin likes about America is Mounds candy bars! They can put it in an ad if they want to, put it on a billboard, [louder] the ONLY thing Charlie Chaplin likes about America is MOUNDS"—his fury at the country which had discarded him was as urgent as the impulses that suddenly turned him into a cat or a tree or a cocktail hostess in mid-conversation.

You could applaud his anger and be captivated by the spurts of pantomime while remaining skeptical about how much money a millionaire needs. Since he obviously adored wealth and property, it was ironic that he was ever called a Communist. (Harold Clurman once told Chaplin that Clifford Odets thought he ought to make a movie "about the 'little man' of *The Gold Rush* after he strikes it rich," about the miseries he would then endure. "'It's not true,' Charlie snapped, 'I like being rich.' The point was that Chaplin had fulfilled himself through money and Odets hadn't.") At times Chaplin behaved with the winsomeness and bathos that marred the weaker scenes in his movies. A ten-year-old remarked, "Yesterday we saw Charlie in *The Gold Rush*. He was funny. Today we saw him at Frognal. He wasn't funny."

Naturally it was disturbing to feel ambivalence toward a genius who had been castigated for his politics. Yet it was instructive to realize that a great artist could be a naïf and a despot. Chaplin often spoke of himself in the third person and he loved to repeat that traffic had stopped on Broadway during his visit to New York in 1916, when a newspaper headline simply announced "HE'S HERE!" Frognal listened politely to that story, which most had heard several times before, while Chaplin kept asking others if they could imagine how exciting that acclaim had been—"Have you ever known anything like it? Have you? Have you?"—and a few celebrities would murmur tactful denials.

If anyone made a joke he was unlikely to laugh. As he rambled away, he sounded more like an anarchist than a socialist; I remember him talking about an ideal society where people would walk into stores and help themselves to anything they wanted; they wouldn't need money because everything would be free. Graham Greene had published a strong statement of support for Chaplin when the Immigration Service moved against him, and the novelist had praised Chaplin's films for compassion "towards the weak and the underprivileged." But I was present when Greene fled Frognal early on one Sunday afternoon "because I couldn't bear to hear Chaplin talking such rot about politics." Yet most of his hearers were indulgent, since they knew what he had suffered in virtual expulsion.

A former story editor at Paramount subsequently told me about a Hollywood benefit in 1950 where Chaplin had paid tribute to Harry Bridges, president of the International Longshoremen's and Warehousemen's Union, for his courage in facing a prison sentence. Chaplin said that if he was ever threatened with jail, he would leave the United States, that he could not remain in prison for a single night, that he would die the minute the cell door closed on him, that he would not be able to breathe, that he would suffocate, that he would not be able to live. He became so agitated that he uttered the same phrases over and over again.

In the summer of 1956 Jane Howard and a couple of her friends arranged a small dinner for the Chaplins to celebrate the completion of the filming of *A King in New York*. But the evening was premature: one short take was still required, a shot of Chaplin walking out of a movie theater. It would be quick work, so Oona Chaplin invited the guests to come to Leicester Square and be extras, standing in line to form a ticket queue. We piled into cars—and arrived in time for a ferocious scene.

The movie camera had been hidden under a sheet in a taxi just outside the cinema: elaborate precautions had been taken so that no one would guess that filming was about to occur. But the sheet fell off the camera. It was a warm Saturday night and a huge crowd suddenly gathered: word spread rapidly that Chaplin was inside the theater and soon several hundred people were massed around the entrance. We found Chaplin having a tantrum in the lobby: he screamed at everyone in sight and vowed to fire the technicians he held responsible. He also refused to shoot the scene that night.

Oona pleaded gently that all he needed to do was to ask the spectators to move back, stressing that they'd be glad to do him any kind of favor—while he sneered at the "fools" and "bastards" outside, contemptuous of the plebeian movie-goers who now jammed the street and much of Leicester Square. It was a very friendly throng, full of Cockney accents; waving and tapping on the glass doors—"Hello, Charlie," "Hey there, tramp!"—they thought he was one of their own: as his movies and public statements had always told them. But he stamped out scowling and shoved his way to his car: it was beneath him to acknowledge or even nod at his beaming audience.

And they got the message. Separated from my friends, I was trapped among the bodies on the pavement, and it was the first time I'd witnessed that moment when an amiable crowd turns angry: muttering about his haughtiness, "His Highness," they knew they'd been insulted. The mood was hostile and briefly I was nervous. Hypocrisy wears many garments, but I could never again hear Chaplin talk tenderly about "the Little Fellow" or "the little people" without recalling how he had disowned the class from which he came, for which he claimed to be a spokesman.

Dinner afterward was dismal; everyone had been upset by Chaplin's behavior and few were skillful at hiding it. Conscious of his exhaustion and his age, we stared at our food while he ranted about the alleged inefficiency of his staff, the stupidity of film fans. The evening crawled along until it was finally rescued by the poet Laurie Lee, who dissolved the constraint by singing Spanish ballads and "On Top of Old Smokey" with his guitar. Lee, a witty troubadour, possessed all the personal charm that Chaplin lacked. Lee's songs inspired Chaplin to parody a Kabuki dancer and we all cheered up a bit.

When *A King in New York* was released in 1957 it proved to be a clumsy attempt to spoof the Committee; between some bewitching passages of mime, Chaplin managed to caricature his own convictions. As the king of a nameless country who loses his throne because he opposes nuclear weapons and plans to use atomic energy for peaceful purposes, he escapes to Manhattan only to discover that America is insane. He's shocked to learn that Americans have to perform debasing tasks in order to make money. Yet the movie oozes with Chaplin's awe of the rich: the camera ogles opulence. His son Michael, aged ten, was cast as a radical prodigy spouting Marx while the indignant king tries to reason with him, and the child's rhetoric becomes a diatribe against all forms of government.

Chaplin crammed his own views beteeen the boy's jaws—and deliberately made them sound foolish. Characterizing the child as a pathetic monster hardly struck a blow for liberalism. The result is oddly reactionary, since the king who defied the Committee was presented as a ridiculous, ineffective figure. But the fact that even Chaplin couldn't make guilt by association comic was essential to the history of the Fifties.

For years the film industry called *A King in New York* "the forbidden comedy"; no major American distributor wanted to handle it, and there were cautious references to its "controversial" content. Chaplin didn't allow the movie to be shown in the United States until 1973; he said earlier offers from independent distributors would merely have earned "peanuts."

Only once did I see Chaplin looking like Chaplin. I was walking along Piccadilly with Don Stewart, the son of DOS, while dense traffic was stalled to a standstill, when we noticed a long limousine that was parallel to us; in the back, huddled on the gleaming seat, was a small bunched solitary figure with its cheek resting on one hand—within that elegant vehicle, his pose distilled all the moments of dejection that trickle though his movies. He did seem to be the Tramp: isolated in unlikely grandeur. Then he saw us and sprang into wild animation, grinning and waving violently. The next day he explained that he'd had an agonizing toothache and was on his way to the dentist. He seemed defensive about having been seen when he looked so despondent. So I felt it would be wrong to say that glimpse of him had moved me.

At Frognal the attitudes of prosperous radicals were sometimes perplexing. Surrounded by archaeological treasures and Paul Klee's paintings, one didn't detect many echoes of the Marxist conviction that the capitalist system degrades all humanity—even though DOS had attacked and burlesqued the capitalist mentality in several of his plays. I didn't doubt his esteem for so-cialism. But Frognal scolded no one for being wealthy.

DOS recalled leaving a Hollywood benefit with another left-wing screenwriter; walking out of a sumptuous mansion they agreed that "We have nothing to lose but our shekels." (Deaf to the Marxist imagery, Ella interrupted: "You know what killed the American Left? They never, *ever* did anything without charging for it! They asked people to benefits who couldn't af-ford them.") I also remember Ella extolling the Chinese for "dig-ging dams with teaspoons," lauding their austerity and then breaking off to rebuke a child for helping herself to a pear from a vast centerpiece. Yet the Stewarts continued to arrange fund-raising events for the international Left, just as they had in Holly-wood, where parties for the Anti-Nazi League or the North American Committee to Aid Spanish Democracy were central to the radical social calendar.

The food at Frognal could be terrible: old shepherd's pie, dank moussaka, gray pâté. Confronted by a dish of moldy beans, some children cried, "But we had that two weeks ago!" Peering into the refrigerator and seeing slime on the leftovers, Eileen O'Casey "thought we'd all be poisoned." Wine from half-empty bottles was often poured into one decanter and served anew; Ella rarely drank, so she didn't think others would notice. "Living well"— in the tradition of DOS's friends Gerald and Sara Murphy— didn't seem to mean eating decently.

Some years would pass before I digested all that I heard at Frognal. Meanwhile I had started to learn a few things about the British welfare state. When I came down with a mild case of viral hepatitis, I didn't go to a doctor because I thought I couldn't af-ford to; at home my parents were deeply in debt because of my mother's ongoing mental and physical illnesses. Then a London friend sent me to his physician, who explained the National Health Service. Walking away from the doctor's office through a thick tawny fog, I was amazed to realize that medical care could be considered a right, not a privilege. And my relief on receiving affordable treatment released all my stored anger at the American medical system.

Throughout my mother's breakdowns and accidents, ambulances kept taking her to Bellevue Hospital during the final years of her life. She was once in the violent ward, then in the psychiatric ward, usually in a general ward. Bellevue became my university as much as Harvard: a large part of my education took place there. I had seen the contempt with which the poor were treated—and how middle-income families became poor when medical costs swallowed all their earnings and savings. I saw how patients became objects. On entering Bellevue you passed a huge sign: CASUALTIES SORTED HERE; often I wondered when a bus or a train wreck would require the disentangling of limbs and torsos beneath the sign. I came to recognize the stink of different wards: through a long maze of corridors I learned to turn right or left at an odor—ether or ammonia or some mysterious reek— though the smell of pea soup and old urine was pervasive. Sometimes I rode in elevators with moaning inmates strapped down on trolleys—had they just had electroshock?—who seemed semi-conscious of pain but not of the orderlies joking and giggling above their heads. In certain other hospitals the patients' cries and wounds were their own business, but in a Bellevue ward the stumps of thighs or arms were as public as the groans; you heard desperate pleas for painkillers that seemed long overdue. When a patient suddenly vomited, the orderlies were apt to fight about whose job it was to clean up—depending on whether the bed or the floor had been soiled. A friend said to me that privacy was the only luxury of the poor. At Bellevue the patients' misery appeared to be increased by all the suffering around them.

There were some fine doctors and a few were sensitive as well as skilled. But others resented a relative's questions and their irritation indicated that people who ended up in Bellevue did not merit much thought: they were rubble, casualties perhaps, but they didn't deserve much more than sorting. The poor were guilty—and so was anyone without enough money for private care. In the Fifties poverty was supposed to belong to the past, to the Depression. Those who had mismanaged their lives or lost control of them had also lost the right to dignity—or even health (or maybe existence): that was one of the lessons of Bellevue.

My mother had flourished in the Twenties and early Thirties, a successful journalist before my birth; at *The New York World* she had covered the Hall-Mills murder trial of 1926 and other subjects rarely assigned to a woman. In the Fifties she had lost touch with her former self and living in the present was intolerable for her; she only wanted her agony to end. Then or now, I could not describe her "character," since severe depression governed much of her conduct once she reached middle age. So we were not close: the span and the violence of her illness had built barriers that we could rarely cross. But affection or intimacy hardly mattered in the context of Bellevue. Someone you loved, or someone you barely knew, or someone you didn't love: all assumed an equal weight within those wards. The emergencies that brought patients to Bellevue and the punishments dispensed by the hospital overwhelmed the nature of any relationship. Friend or stranger, favorite sibling or family albatross: they were all humiliated there, reduced to breathing or dying debris. I didn't expect my mother to be cured. She was eventually diagnosed as manic-depressive and the doctors were hazy about treatment. As she journeyed back to Bellevue between long stays in other hospitals—Columbia Presbyterian and Bloomingdale's in White Plains and Goldwater Memorial Hospital on Welfare Island—until her "remains" were delivered to the Bellevue morgue for an autopsy, I learned that there were no solutions for the sick unless they had limitless funds.

I didn't know then that my anger had any relation to politics or social systems; no one had yet said that the personal could be political. But in England I saw how certain kinds of equality could be legislated. Occasionally I heard a Frognal guest say that Britain's welfare state was merely an exercise in reform, that the Labour Party hadn't advanced socialism. But those remarks couldn't diminish my respect for a program designed for anyone who was ill.

The contrast between Bellevue and a national health plan showed me that an aesthete could not dwell apart from politics, that what happened to one's body had a lot to do with the mind and soul. My perspective wouldn't jell until the Sixties, but what I listened to at Frognal would give me a background for the future as well as the past.

When the exiles were together, there were fond references to Tim Costello's saloon on Third Avenue and to hearing jazz at Eddie Condon's, and DOS was excited by the prospect of following the World Series on special broadcasts at the American embassy. And I thought they were probably as homesick as I was—since the need to be with other Americans drew us back to Frognal week after week. I was keen to hear further tales of Columbus, Ohio, where my father and DOS had been raised, along with the folklore of Manhattan and Hollywood; at Frognal I touched base with tangibilities that I missed more and more.

As for London, one could easily be charmed by a leafy city of verbal wit where no one was an eccentric. But like many generations of my compatriots, I first discovered my national identity by living abroad. After two years I pined for New York until my hunger for its physical details was almost absurd. I longed to see great ugly chocolate rabbits in Fifth Avenue windows at Easter. From a distance I tried to visualize the view of the Con Edison smokestacks that appears when you sit on the steps of the Public Library. The infectious energy that seems to leap from the sidewalks, the scents of my Yorkville block, where—halfway between the brewery and the Necco wafer factory—you could sniff the switch from beer to candy when the wind changed, the whole scope of incongruities that characterize the city, and many friends: memories of these could tighten the throat of an infrequent weeper. Dreaming again and again of sauntering beneath the Third Avenue El in summer, watching the soot swirl down through the sunlight when a train passed overhead, I grieved for a landscape already demolished and grew possessive of that grief because the English couldn't share it.

Craving a glimpse of the Triborough Bridge or a flock of bright yellow taxis, I went to third-rate American movies just because they were shot in New York. And I kept returning to revivals of the best ones. When I needed to hear the voices of my town, I was gratified when Marlon Brando sighed, "I coulda been a contender" in *On the Waterfront* or when Tony Curtis snarled, "I'm nice to people when it pays me to be nice!" in *Sweet Smell of Success*. Hankering for American landscapes I'd never seen, I also sat through many Westerns, which used to bore me. One evening I found the poet and playwright William Alfred—who was on a sabbatical from Harvard—standing alone in a line for the movie of *Oklahoma!*: he'd been in London barely a month, but he was feeling as misplaced as I was. Often I recalled the blazing oranges, reds, and yellows of an upstate New York fall during the tame mists of an English autumn, when clumps of wet leaves slowly turned black and rotted off the dripping branches. I writhed when British actors mangled the accents in the plays of Eugene O'Neill and Tennessee Williams, trying to mimic Americans by using imbecilic drawls. I guarded my own accent: nothing could induce me to pronounce the *h* in *herb* or to ignore the *c* in *schedule*. Nor would I call an elevator a lift or a dessert a sweet: stubborn in fidelity to my language, I was ashamed of visiting Americans who said "Cheerio" instead of "Good-bye."

Toward the end of five years in London I lived on Cheyne Walk in an apartment where the Thames was reflected in the mirrors on the walls. My desk faced the river. But the waters seemed dead: only a few houseboats and some listless swans rocked slowly on the gray tides below me, and I yearned for the turbulent life of the East River, where steamers and tugs and cargo ships and garbage scows churn past the John Finley Walk. That was *my* river: I had walked along it to school each day, been kissed for the first time looking at the lights on the opposite shore; I knew it blue in the summer, silvery in winter, always changing and tumbling and rippling, and once I saw it partly frozen after a great blizzard.

In London, between the moments when my mind raced along the East River or exulted in the bridges that swing between Manhattan and Queens, I reread *The Waste Land* and felt I had a fresh insight into Eliot's choice of the Thames as a symbol for the moribund nature of England: "Unreal City, / Under the brown fog of a winter dawn, / A crowd flowed over London Bridge, so many, / I had not thought death had undone so many." Of course Eliot chose London and the Thames as images of sterility in all contemporary culture. But unfairly I saw that dull water as a metaphor for what the English criticized in their own society, especially the conventions that lingered from earlier eras. Actually the late Fifties was a time of vitality in England: the arts and the economy were thriving, along with all kinds of dissent. But in my appetite for my country and my city, I'd come to feel that London had little to offer anyone who wasn't English.

Missing the immigrant culture of New York, I found it strange not to hear Yiddish; the English didn't know what was meant by *kvetching* or *schmoozing*; there seemed to be no equivalent to the drive that carried émigrés from the Lower East Side and Brooklyn to Carnegie Hall or Tin Pan Alley, to City College and Columbia, to the pages of *Partisan Review*. New York was a Jewish city—to the extent that a non-Jew could absorb traditions that weren't instilled from birth. Although London welcomed intellects from many countries, most of its districts from Pimlico to Hampstead seemed almost entirely British, even though you could see yarmulkes or turbans in a few of them. But I was accustomed to ethnicity of all sorts, to bagels and gefilte fish, tamales and tostadas, the dumplings of Mott Street. The Poles and Russians and Hispanics and Italians of my city—whose idiom enlivened the speech heard all over town—were part of its mainstream, whereas the Indians, Jamaicans, and Cypriots living in London in the Fifties didn't have much influence on its language or its customs; it wasn't yet the multi-racial city it would become in the Eighties.

Alfred Kazin wrote that Scott Fitzgerald "took American history as *his* history," and so did I: I felt a connection with events and people long preceding my birth, even while I was strolling beside the Thames. The American euphoria at the end of World War I and the triumphant sense of independence from Europe, the high spirits of the Twenties, the anguish of the Depression: all that belonged to me—in a way that distanced me from most of the Brits I knew. So I sympathized with the Irish, the Welsh, and the Scots who refused to be assimilated, who rebelled with gusto against the English.

I was hardly an irretrievable expatriate; only the fact that I married an Englishman prevented me from walking down York Avenue or across Eighty-sixth Street. But as I learned more about exiles throughout history, I allied myself with those who had had to leave their countries, either because they were thrust out or had needed to escape. From the German Jews to Americans who had been stripped of their passports, I identified with people who couldn't see or smell their own neighborhoods, couldn't visit the local delicatessen or trade jokes at the news stand or hear their own vernacular. A character in *The Caucasian Chalk Circle*— which Brecht wrote while he was living in America—says, "Why does one love one's country? Because the bread tastes better there, the sky is higher, the air is spicier, voices ring out more clearly, the ground is softer to walk on."

Most of my British friends thought such emotions ludicrous. But it is difficult for the expatriate to convey the intensity of those feelings or to legitimize the sadness that accompanies them. Years later I was told that wartime refugees from Berlin and Prague and Budapest used to weep over their desserts at Yaddo, the artists' colony in Saratoga, when the Bavarian pastry chef made the tortes or soufflés of their hometowns. The spectacle of middle-aged writers and composers in tears over the whipped cream was astonishing to onlookers who'd been impressed by their self-control in larger spheres. But often it is the most prosaic item which triggers a sense memory—releasing a gust of deprivation that runs beyond the rational.

The Frognal community was more fortunate than some: their affinities had moved to London when they did; their luggage included shared pain and slang. Yet I noticed that while they dwelled on the past and lived very much in the present, they seemed to have little sense of the future—perhaps because they didn't know if they would ever be able to see their own country again: in the mid-Fifties there could be no certainty of that, and some of them were approaching sixty. When Arthur Miller's adaptation of Ibsen's *An Enemy of the People* was performed on British television in 1957 and the besieged "revolutionist" said, "We'll go to America"—where life would be freer than in his neo-fascist town—the Frognal guests whooped and slapped their thighs. At the same time most felt they were "the real Americans": proud of their participation in the Thirties, proud of their refusal to tolerate the Cold War inquisitions, they asserted that an American had the right to hold any opinion, to vote as he wished or to express unpopular views. For them the Committee was un-American—even treasonous, since it betrayed the country's best legacies—and they were the patriots.

"Have you got the little green book?": in those days American passports were green, and in 1958 the exiles began to ask one another that eager question, then to brandish the passports that had been restored at last—usually after prolonged legal exertions. When Leonard Boudin won back the passport of the artist Rockwell Kent in a 1957 landmark case and the Supreme Court ruled that passports could not be withheld for political reasons, many others then regained theirs through similar litigation. DOS happily showed me the passport he received just before his sixty-third birthday. At the bar of the American embassy he held a small wake for his blacklist pseudonym, toasting the death of Gilbert Holland. Once again it was possible to revisit or even live in the United States. All over London the elation was contagious. Rarely have passport photographs displayed such a range of triumphant smiles.

In the Frognal garden Paul Robeson was embraced by jubilant blacklistees soon after his passport was returned, and W. E. B. Du Bois called on DOS and Ella when he was permitted to travel. But few foresaw that blacklisting would persist well into the Sixties. Although Otto Preminger openly hired Dalton Trumbo to write *Exodus* in 1960, almost no one else fared as well. Albert Maltz did not receive a screen credit until 1964—after sixteen years on the blacklist. Abraham Polonsky had to write anonymously for nearly two decades. Ring Lardner's name didn't appear on the screen until 1965. In that same year Lester Cole of the Hollywood Ten had to use a pseudonym for *Born Free*: even so, Columbia had balked at retaining any part of his script when the executives realized who had written it. (They did so only at Carl Foreman's insistence.) Cole had worked as a waiter, as a short-order cook, and in a warehouse while he was blacklisted. Nedrick Young, an actor and occasional screenwriter who co-wrote *The Defiant Ones,* became a bartender. Elliott Sullivan and Anne Revere—Gregory Peck's mother in *Gentleman's Agreement* and Elizabeth Taylor's in *National Velvet*—were barred from movies until 1969. Pete Seeger was not allowed on a sponsored television network between 1950 and 1967, and Larry Adler still could not perform on any sponsored show in the Seventies. Many others were too old or too far out of touch to reenter the industry; some careers could never be recovered.

Hence quite a few exiles, like DOS and Ella Winter, continued to reside abroad; they would return briefly to the United States only when a grandchild was born or if their memoirs were published. But the pain and fear and fury that had governed the Fifties had also destroyed many intimate friendships, which could never be resumed: in that realm few of the exiles could regain the lives they had known before the blacklist. Charlie Chaplin thought he could never go back to America. And an abhorrence of the Left lingered on among countless American liberals, who kept deploring the dead McCarthy as a phenomenon, an abberant personality, but were equally contemptuous of those who had been reviled. So the little green book provided an entrée only to carefully chosen company, to certain altering landscapes—but it was not valid for travel to Hungary or Bulgaria or to some ruined chapters of the American past.

# VI.

A plum pudding was responsible for my marriage. Two years earlier, just before I separated from the young American who'd been at Oxford, his father and brother arrived in London in mid-December. The forlorn father, in the midst of a divorce, seemed to be hoping to hear that we were engaged; instead he was told we were parting. He'd come to see us to be cheered up; now he was depressed. For Christmas he gave me a gigantic plum pudding from Fortnum & Mason; since we were having the holiday dinner at Brown's Hotel, he didn't expect me to serve it. But he'd bought the thing before he knew his son and I were breaking up, and I sensed that it was meant to be the cornerstone of a house.

Each time I moved, the pudding went with me. That big red box stood on shelves or in the bottom of closets: seeing it made me a bit sad. Someone had trusted me to make a man happy; together he and I had betrayed that trust. I didn't regret our severance, but I couldn't abandon the pudding—that would have felt like hurting the father all over again.

Aware that it improved with age, that it became a greater delicacy each month, I tried to give it to a series of Londoners. But they refused it. Either they disliked heavy desserts or they rarely cooked, or else they hated Christmas or despised the British institutions that the pudding seemed to symbolize: the royal family, the Anglican church. Then Mai Zetterling's Danish friends returned to Kensington Court and received it with cries of enthusiasm. But they forgot to take it with them; a friend drove me speedily to the airport in their wake, the pudding bouncing on the back seat. We caught up with them but it made their luggage overweight so they had to pass it back to me. By then the red box seemed like the albatross in *The Ancient Mariner*.

A year had passed. I offered it to John Davenport and he said it would be splendid for his family on Boxing Day. As I gratefully handed the pudding to him in his favorite pub, he asked me to join them for that upcoming holiday. I looked forward to seeing his home: Rossetti's studio in Flood Street (Henry James had called it "the most delicious melancholy old House of Chelsea"). But I heard nothing more from him, so on Boxing Day I phoned a mutual friend who said Davenport's wife was ill and guests were out of the question. I was very disappointed; after the exhilaration of the Zetterling-Power Christmas, I wanted the festivities to continue. All my housemates had left London; I was alone in Flat Seven, which was strewn with gold paper and silver ribbons. It was cold: drafts seeped from the corners. The lights flickered and dimmed, and there were no more candles. Then a stranger rang, an editorial writer for *The Daily Telegraph*; he'd heard about the Davenport short circuit and invited me to his house for a dinner party. Singing "Jubilate Deo," I flung on a bright red dress, drenched myself in Schiaparelli's Shocking and ran out to find a taxi: now Christmas would last forever.

At my host's cozy home, I met a fashion reporter from the European edition of *The New York Times*; call her Maria. She had narrowed eyes, a bony nose, dark hair pulled back in a chignon, and wore an elegantly simple wool dress with a fur collar. She was in her early thirties, sleek and purposeful; the precision with which she crossed her legs and smoked was enviable. I was startled to hear from her voice that she was American. She had a wry Yankee accent, nasal and half-defiant. At moments she held back her breath and sounded husky. Chic as she was, she sometimes talked like Salinger's Holden Caulfield—"for Chrissake," "strictly for the birds"—or in the tone of a dead-end kid. (At a later time she assumed a grand ultra-English accent instead of her tough street style.)

Soon she had everyone laughing. Declaring that the British don't pronounce English correctly, she described sitting next to "a stuffy Foreign Office type" at a dinner party; he inquired, "Does one sacrifice lust from May to December?" Riled by his pompous manner, she gave him a long, raunchy answer—which included throwing vestal virgins into the sea—as he looked more and more alarmed. He said he'd heard that she had lived in Burma and he timidly repeated his question—"Does one sack of rice last from May to December?"—because his sister had recently sent him one from there and he wanted to know how long it would be before he needed another.

As we left she said she would call me: "There's a man I want you to meet." That annoyed me—not only because matchmakers are apt to be greedy for power but because a couple of them had introduced me to tiresome men who were hard to escape. I'd learned to treat the plotters with casual indifference: if one resisted, they tightened the pressure. I'd liked Maria but soon she became a nag, phoning me frequently about this economist (ugh), and after stalling for nearly three months I agreed to come to her house and then dine with them, simply to get it over with. I expected a ham-fisted, greasy creep. Sour breath, probably no chin.

To my surprise he was attractive—a steep forehead that wrinkled when he laughed, a smile that cut high into his cheeks, a short upper lip—but I was suspicious: it was plain that he and Maria knew each other well and she seemed to want him for herself, so what was I doing there? Was she planning a threesome? His eyebrows were bushy; she plucked out a hair or two while he protested: it looked like a ritual. From their conversation I gathered that he had many ex-girlfriends; she ridiculed them, along with a couple of older women who had pursued him: "Lie down, young man." She also mimicked the posh inflections of a mutual acquaintance who had solemnly quoted Melanie Klein's theories of the good breast and the bad breast; they chuckled together.

Complaining of an ear infection that made her feel as if she were in a cave of the winds, Maria told him to raise his voice, so he did, but not too loudly. Considerate, I thought. Over a quick meal at a Chelsea restaurant they talked rapidly to one another while I listened politely, wishing the evening were at an end. Still, I liked the way he ate cold asparagus, his long fingers dragging each stalk slowly through the sauce. I also liked the way his shoulders moved when he walked. Once he spoke to me directly, asking what I would have been doing if I weren't there. I said I was in the London Bach Group; normally we would have been rehearsing motets for a Bach festival, but the rehearsal had been cancelled. He seemed to find that odd.

Driving him to the airport for a Swiss skiing holiday, we stopped to pick up a woman who was going with him. Maria bristled. I relaxed: this was getting funny. Realizing that I was the only one who was at ease and that somebody should make conversation, I said I thought one should always have a bowl of oyster stew before a journey. The new woman—jovial but extremely uncomfortable—turned to me thankfully: "I think so too!" But how could that be? I was referring to the Oyster Bar in Grand Central Station, where my parents had bought me oyster stew before I returned to boarding school in Vermont. Well, she'd been in New York and had eaten that stew in the station; she had known students at my school. Maria snorted. He said to her, "Isn't she *young*!," which irritated me. After that he was silent, but at the airport he suddenly said to me, "Keep singing until I come back!" I thought that was presumptuous.

On the way home Maria told me that they'd lived with each

other for about two years, had almost married, but she'd left him for a philosopher—a dapper positivist who excelled at the samba, was said to be a charmer, and was perpetually on the sniff for other women. Maria reflected, "You have to keep a man on a very long rope," and I recoiled from the image: it sounded like captivity or strangulation. As for the woman we'd taken to the airport, that was merely "a disentangling affair" between people who were recovering from others. Maria spoke wistfully about her former lover, and I wondered if she might have been using me as bait: to coax him under her roof. I was glad to be free of both of them when I got home to Kensington Court. Again I remembered E. M. Forster's "odors from the abyss": these two seemed to reek of trouble.

I forgot about them for a fortnight, immersed in reading plays by Giraudoux and Molnár. Tyrone Power was filming in Mexico, Mai was on her everlasting tour with *La Sauvage*; I was missing part of my tribe. One morning Louis and Etienne woke me too early by quarreling noisily, then they spilled so much sugar on the linoleum floor of the kitchen that bare feet got sticky and shoes crunched horribly: the day began with walking on sugar. I spoke harshly to them, calling them inconsiderate, and they burst into convulsive tears. Amid their sobs I answered the phone; it was the economist, just back from Switzerland: would I be free for dinner tonight? At another time I would have pretended to be busy, but I felt guilty about the weeping children, so I said yes. When I hung up they were still crying and I apologized—but why were they so dreadfully upset? Louis gasped, "You said we were *inconsiderate*—and we don't know what it means."

That evening swept me into a new chapter of my life, after we confessed how wary we'd been of one another, how we'd both avoided meeting. But Maria had been right in guessing that our resistance would dissolve in person. Still, she was furious to learn that we'd spent Easter weekend together, and she came storming into Flat Seven when I was beginning breakfast. Because the coffee pot was broken and I wanted plenty of coffee, I was struggling with a row of six small café filtres: that enraged her because it was comic. I was wearing a long flowing red flannel gown, a rather papal garment; Maria glared and said it was good that I was dressed for a big scene.

With a contorted face she ordered me to stop seeing him—apparently titillated by jealousy, she wanted him back—and followed me to my bedroom, where I was unpacking a suitcase. She hissed, "You're young and it's spring and that's *all* you have to offer." (I wrote that down because I feared it might be true. Yet I still believed that youth was a disadvantage, and at twenty-four I wanted to be older.) In a rage she wept, tearing matchboxes to shreds, then hurled herself down on my bed and threatened suicide. Her ex-husband was very ill, she said; how would I feel if her small daughter became an orphan?

But as she shouted through her tears, I didn't believe she would kill herself. (The phrase "too mean to die" slid into my mind, but I tried to banish it.) She was triumphant about suffering and that made me angry. I thought she was half-crazed but also that she loved making horrific scenes—and that her kind of temporary madness could be contagious, that she might help to drive others mad. And I was shocked because she seemed to have no pride.

Yet by assaulting us, by tossing emotional grenades in our path, she brought us closer to one another. The man in question dealt calmly with her demands, he kept her at a distance. But he and his friends couldn't stop talking about her; she was equally fascinating and frightening, and I wasn't allowed to think she belonged to history. I remembered Rebecca, a figure of immense power although she was no longer loved. As I kept hearing about what Maria had said and done, I felt overwhelmed by her enormous shadow, and at times it seemed as if she were living with us—with her flashing eyes, her live-wire jokes, her elegance and violence. I thought the past could drain life out of the present and even menace the future: by implying that it might repeat the past.

And yet happiness surged over my doorsill along with that witty, outgoing man who was eight years older than I; he challenged my concepts of privacy and freedom: he said they could be shared. Looking out the bay window of Flat Seven, four floors above the ground, I would see his white car tearing into Kensington Court and screeching to a halt before he ran across the street and up the stairs to be with me. We went dancing all over London, now and then at the Gargoyle, a seedy Soho club with a glittering wall mosaic made of tiles cut from antique mirrors, whistled the curtain-raising waltz from *La Sauvage* (a tune as bewitching as "La Ronde"), and had sex whenever and wherever we could: in borrowed apartments (so Louis and Etienne wouldn't hear—we were noisy in bed), in country fields, once in a ditch off the highway.

I came to think that the best orgasms bring whatever you see up close, as a zoom lens does. We made fun of the sex scenes in Hemingway: the lovers' baby talk in *A Farewell to Arms* and the earth moving in *For Whom the Bell Tolls.* Yet in an unstable, treacherous world—or so I perceived it—everything seemed firm as well as joyful when he was inside me. One afternoon a pigeon came flapping down a chimney in a room where we were making love; it seemed like a mysterious visitation, not that we believed in the Holy Ghost. Talking, snoozing, slipping into sex again, we didn't mean to stay up all night, but sometimes we saw the wrong end of the dawn, when the buildings outside our window were edged in dull pink.

In our first months, high spirits traveled with us. We went to Brighton and rode through a little tunnel of horrors, where shabby skeletons sprang out at us and the recorded screams were faint. One night, finding an empty carousel by a roadside, we spun around until the music stopped. He was addicted to oysters and we pursued them throughout Soho and the City, in seafood bars and French bistros. He introduced me to hock, and we drank it with ice and soda, as Oscar Wilde had before his arrest at the Cadogan Hotel. We traded the humor of our two countries; he explained Cockney rhyming slang: china for a close friend, a mate (china plate), Bristols (Bristol cities meant titties), trouble and strife (wife), and I told him knock-knock jokes: "Fornication like this we need champagne." In the white car we sang old music-hall songs: "I used to think that he was my young man, / He used to call me his lit-tle Ma-ry Ann, / Till Mother caught his eye and they got married on the sly, / And now I have to call him Fa-ther."

Living in the present, the moment, our days were also flavored with anticipation: what would we do tomorrow or next week? Ride polo ponies—for only ten shillings apiece—in Richmond Park? Listen to a debate in the House of Commons? (Occasionally he considered standing for Parliament, and some of his friends liked to imagine him as Chancellor of the Exchequer, but he had grave doubts about leading a politician's life.) Would we see Kazan's *Face in the Crowd* or Chaplin's *King in New York*? Eat Chinese dumplings on the King's Road or snails at La Bicyclette in Pimlico? (Chelsea's most engaging Indian restaurant had been closed down for serving Kit-E-Kat: we'd been eating curried cat food and loving it.) Stay in all evening and read the books we'd given each other? I gave him Scott Fitzgerald, he gave me George Orwell's essays. Plan a trip to Greece?

Although his field was economics, he didn't seem much interested in money; his family was well-heeled, he'd earned handsomely in his twenties and hence could afford a low salary for work that appealed to him. When his friends asked for financial guidance, he recommended investing in rust-proof paint (for the many new city buildings) and day-old chicks (the rotisserie business was booming). Those stocks thrived and he remarked with amusement that he hadn't bothered to follow his own advice.

Meanwhile I found that traveling with someone can make his habits seem like one's own. Each night he dumped everything in his pockets onto a bureau; coins and keys, business cards, cigarettes, and a minuscule ivory pig would vanish neatly in the morning. Memories of our first season are unleashed by the briny taste of raw oysters, the scent of tall summer grasses on a Wiltshire hill, "The Rain in Spain" over the airwaves, bunches of red and purple anemones like those he brought to Kensington Court.

He was very decisive—I admired that and also shrank from it—and was a fluent story-teller with a strong visual memory. The Treasury, where he'd worked before I knew him, employed many blind typists: during one of London's mammoth fogs, the halls were choked with such thick coils of grayness that the sighted felt their way along the walls; when they heard brisk footsteps, they knew those belonged to the blind. His abundant energies masked a haunting medical history: at twenty he had been told he had a week to live; a kidney damaged in childhood had gone wrong at the end of the war when he was in the RAF. He was sitting alone on a hillside, weeping because there was no future, when a young girl rode by on a horse. As she stared at him, he swallowed his tears. And as the weeks passed, the medics were astounded that he didn't die. (The kidney was removed a few years later; in the hospital bed next to his, a man kept groaning, "My name is De'ath," a common surname in Cambridgeshire.) Soon I shared his aversion to cooked kidneys, learning not to shudder when weekend hosts spoke proudly of the curried/ grilled/sautéed kidneys they'd just prepared, but to be clever at disposal: tossing one swiftly out a window, dropping another into a flower bed. He refused to let almost anything embarrass him, and that seemed to expand his resilience, his self-assurance. He expected people to like him and most did.

We laughed about the chain of consequences that started with the plum pudding: if I'd never received it or if I'd gone to John Davenport's Boxing Day dinner, we wouldn't have met. We

might well have swum past each other like two fish in a river
—fish borne by opposite currents, which will never be in the
same waters again. Still, that was a stretch for him: as an ultra-
rationalist he used to say, "You mustn't write history with ifs"
(which most writers do all the time). We also spoke of touchstones
and tuning forks: images of integrity that made us think of one
another—during a long London spring of flowering chestnuts in
the parks, lilacs rustling in the squares, wisteria blooming on
walls and fences.

Briefly visiting New York, we typed messages to each other
on the small typewriter mounted on a pedestal outside the Oli-
vetti offices on Fifth Avenue. We went to Venice and Vicenza, to
Chicago and West Cornwall, Connecticut. Warned that Venice
was impossible in August and that the Lido would be disgusting,
we basked in that city's beauties and were mesmerized by the
shimmering heat haze on the Lido's beaches. At Vicenza we
roamed through Palladio's Villa Rotunda when no one was there
except a yawning caretaker; a few chickens clucked around us as
we mounted the grand stairs. Chicago was a downer: a bitter aunt
of mine and her sullen married lover kept us apart at night and
took us to a steak restaurant on the edge of an indoor skating
rink: large chips of dirty ice kept landing on our dinner plates.
Connecticut restored our morale: standing shin-deep in the shal-
lows of the Housatonic River, we caught crayfish in the nets we'd
made from our hostess's old hats and veils. In England we went
to a house on an estuary in Devon and to a wide pagan ring of
tall stones at Avebury in Wiltshire. The stones dated back to
around 2500 B.C. on the chalk-filled downs, where skylarks
soared overhead. When we first saw the stones, the sky above and
between them was a pale silvery blue. For the first time I began
to enjoy being young instead of regretting it—because there was
so much of life ahead.

His tales engrossed me and we talked ceaselessly. But did we
really hear what each other was saying? I don't think so. He was

never a listener—far from it—and my attention often strayed, not from his experiences but during his unrelenting monologues: about conraceptives, scuba diving, archaeology, sexual dramas at the United Nations, the Common Market, Venetian glass, Anthony Eden (whom he scorned), French women, carpentry, Queen Victoria's bridal nightgown (he said there was a triangle to unbutton at the crotch), Yugoslavia, skiing, anything. Intriguing subjects, but there were no pauses. He was skilled at telling complicated jokes, some in several accents. Eloquent without effort, he was given to constant interruptions and could control a conversation by cutting others short. So he lived in a world of unfinished sentences that weren't his own: verbal rubble.

He was often patronizing, and with "rationality" as his yardstick he could make anyone's ideas seem absurd: reductio ad absurdum might have been his motto. (When I kept saying I missed New York, he replied that I preferred stones—that is, skyscrapers—to people.) Almost any kind of religion—from Christianity to Zen—was repugnant to him, and he derided his family's tradition of "goddamn Quaker do-gooding." Religious faith was downright nonsensical, particularly for educated people. At worst he made others feel that he thought they were fools. But his style of logic meant that he couldn't be caught in his own traps. With Maria he'd acquired a habit of asking, "Do you love me more than life itself?" I didn't like that and protested that it was impossible to answer. He said it was supposed to be impossible.

The legacy of his years with her persisted. Immensely attractive to all sorts of women, he kept repeating that he could easily make out with X or Y, that Z had come on to him, that former girlfriends were sending erotic signals. One of his male friends exclaimed, "But *you* can't be getting married—you're our long-range ballistic missile!" A man of his vibrant sexuality had no reason to be boastful, but he'd told me that jealousy excited Maria, that she liked him all the more when others wanted him. So he was accustomed to stoking the coals. I wasn't possessive or jealous by nature, so I was not inflamed, I merely felt replaceable, especially because he seemed to love conquest itself.

In the meantime our national differences created gulfs that were difficult to cross. Later on we had a terrific fight about Thoreau's "Civil Disobedience": he was outraged by Thoreau's refusal to pay taxes and I exulted in the defiance of authority, in Thoreau's opposition to slavery and his rebellion against the American war on Mexico. We tried to dwell with our conflicts in terms of our cultures—his support for the socialism of the welfare state, and my identification with fierce Yankee individualism and its distrust of government per se, should not be powerful enough to divide us. (In fact I would value British socialism once I knew more about it.) But he said angrily that Thoreau was stupid and that infuriated me. Our collisions could seem to hinge on our nationalities, but they were symptoms of deeper discords. The rationalist tended to assume that he was more intelligent than anyone who disagreed with him; since your mind wasn't equal to his, he often turned his back in mid-argument while you were talking. Contempt could narrow his eyes and tighten his lips. But when we clashed, sex was the solution: how could anyone do battle after exhilaration between the sheets?

At times feelings flew in all directions. I had already discovered that when you are in love there can be hours (or days) when strangers look like the person who matters most to you: again and again you see him walking toward you on the street, while others on the sidewalk seem more vital than they did before. This is hardly the basis for a marriage, but I caved in after he repeated, "Marry or quit." That was his great error. Because I feared making the wrong decision I made none at all. That was mine.

I didn't want to marry anyone; along with some offspring of disastrous marriages, I believed that being married meant being unhappy and that it brought an end to love. I longed to think that love could last, but because it almost never did I assumed from the start that we would part one day. I thought fragmentation was the nature of life, yet I yearned for continuity while being sure that it was unattainable. I was hugely influenced by others' experiences, probably too much so. Most of the marriages I knew —my parents' and their friends', much of London—had been very destructive; I'd seen a lot of permanent scars among those whose marriages had ruined their lives. I wouldn't have agreed with Schopenhauer that "every life history is a history of suffering," but I saw most husbands and wives as one another's adversaries: they had no basis for trusting each other.

I feared imprisonment, that marriage would be a dungeon. My husband-to-be had also shied away from marriage; now my unwillingness seemed to turn him on. Appalled by the prospect of marrying, I tried to distinguish between rational fears and irrational terrors, but I didn't succeed very well. My whole life was about to change once again, but I didn't realize that I could be in charge of it, that choice could be more consequential than chance.

And of course I had no wish to settle in England, certainly not to become English. London was somewhat less friendly: I was marrying one of the city's most popular bachelors, aggravating the hostesses who wanted him to stay single. And strangers expected wives—even young ones—to be boring. When I thought about the challenges and excitements of New York, I realized that it was a place where (as someone said) you could open yourself to the future. Or reinvent yourself—not that I wanted to, but I liked the idea that many New Yorkers could and did. And I knew that I could lead very different lives there—several at once or others in sequence—rather than one life in London with one person.

As New York's magnetism increased, I kept hearing that someone who looked like me and wore clothes like mine had been sighted in my favorite parts of Manhattan: walking along the East River, listening to folksingers around the fountain in Washington Square, at an off-Broadway theater or in the garden of the Museum of Modern Art. College friends kept calling my parents' apartment and asking to speak to me—they'd seen me at a distance but hadn't been able to catch up with me—and were astonished to hear that I hadn't been there at all. In London I joked about my double while I secretly applauded that unknown self—who went where I wanted to, eluded even well-meaning persons, and could never quite be pinned down. My roots seemed to be sinking even deeper into the flinty soil of my hometown while I was supposed to be committing myself to England.

The man I was about to marry spoke in favor of sexual equality and seemed to believe that it had already been achieved; he said the scarce modern feminists were "chaining themselves to railings that were no longer there." The women's movement was well in the distance, no one I knew saw it coming. He quite often did the dishwashing, which I detested. I don't think we ever talked about the roles of wives—or women or men, or about what family life might be. But much later I learned that he felt wives should mold their lives around their husbands', that work of their own was an "extra." None of that did we discuss, although I kept writing and was enchanted by my first taste of reporting, by the adventures it entailed.

Tyrone Power's wedding gift was the loan of his pretty Abingdon Road house for two months, while he was in California. Amid the framed posters of his Irish great-grandfather's plays, we would be a rum household: Power didn't know that his adoring, wildly neurotic secretary, a woman whose pinched, miserable face was etched with longing, would move into the house to protect the place she held sacred from our profane intrusion. (She wanted everything to be perfect for him, and she'd exasperated him by throwing out his barely-used tubes of toothpaste and shaving cream and replacing them with new ones. He said his bathroom wasn't safe from her.) Grimly she referred to my almost-husband as "your friend" and to my father—who came

over for the wedding—as "your other friend." My father caught
a heavy cold, so he too moved in. The secretary took so many long
baths that we could rarely have any. Water rushed and gurgled
through the pipes most of the day and much of the night, and my
father said she was an "ondinist." Her wrathful, waterlogged
presence made the beginning of marriage seem surreal. When I
hear water running through a building's walls, it revives a jum-
ble of emotions: romantic love, dread of marriage, fierce resent-
ment (at having been pressured to marry), self-scorn (for having
yielded, for seeming spineless), a childish desire to escape, a wist-
ful impulse to stay close to my husband, to savor our intimacy.
Wanting to be with him and to flee from him, while a sentence
kept racing through my mind: "One day you'll *have* to let me go!"

Power and Mai had bridled their instincts and managed not to
ask if I knew what I was doing, but I saw that each was on the
brink of that question. I would not have forgiven them if they
had asked. Mai was newly involved with David Hughes, the
English novelist she would marry the following year. She was
starring in a Swedish film of Strindberg's anti-feminist satire of
*A Doll's House,* but she flew back from Stockholm to be a witness
at our wedding in the Chelsea Registry Office. Beforehand, as I
dressed in Power's sunny bedroom and peered into the three-
sided mirror, I thought of those movies where the bride is rescued at the altar by Cary Grant or some other upstart who
prevents the nuptials. I wore a sleeveless velvet sheath with a pattern of dark red roses on a strawberry background, crimson
suede stiletto heels, sheer faintly red stockings which suggested a
mild sunburn. I've always loved red, but that day it was worn for
courage.

At the reception, held in a house in Bayswater, the host's elderly father asked me the names of several guests and then said
with a far-away smile, "What a pity this isn't a kitchen party for
one's staff. Then one would know all the names and whom to

tip." Before the reception we had returned to Kensington Court for glasses of Russian tea, and as Louis and Etienne threw grains of rice at us I wondered how anyone could foresee the next curve in the river; I kept thinking how a swimmer could be carried away by the tide. What if the tide was love? Might that transport you—eventually—to some kind of safety on the shore?

# Afterward

Sometimes I wake in vanished rooms. I'm there just as a dream recedes, at that moment before one recognizes one's actual surroundings. I often remember what I saw as the day began, during earlier chapters of my life—in places where I'll never be again. In my Queen's Gate bed-sitter the gas ring was right next to the washstand; I stared at them while I made plans about looking for work. In Blomfield Road the Regency bedroom had wallpaper with pale lemon-and-white stripes; the propriety of the decor reminded me of Arthur Koestler's chintz and his Courbet cow: a formal setting for his wildest rages. At times I woke anxious about the scenes he might make in the days ahead. In Bourne Street my bed faced a narrow window that was my weather report: my spirits sank or rose as the panes revealed a bank of yellowish-brown fog or a light-blue day. My expectations were low, but—fog or no fog—my life was about to improve. At Kensington Court my eyes opened on a scarred dartboard; by the age of nine Louis had lost interest in that target, but it still hung on the wall of his former bedroom. Being in a child's room gave me an odd sense of stability, a feeling that I had many years to live. From my marital bed on Cheyne Walk we could see the steaming smoke stacks of the Lots Road Power Station—a notorious polluter—across the Thames; it looked as though it belonged in one of Whistler's portraits of the river. Like A. J. Liebling I've had many homes, and in my sleep they reappear, almost as palpable as the present.

Those awakenings in those rooms seem like a chronicle of a life in progress. I think our early twenties are just as influential as childhood in shaping our natures and futures, our reflexes, our pleasures and our fears. Doris Lessing wrote in her autobiography, "I believe the need to learn is the most powerful passion we have," and while I can't go quite that far, I know how very greedy a learner can be. That was what sent me abroad, spurred by an appetite which long before had led Henry James to keep writing about "a certain young woman affronting her destiny." I think my destiny was what I learned—not that education ever ceases.

Adventurous Americans could find that we were freer than many Europeans to range among cultures that were hardly acquainted with one another; we could easily feel at home in the world at large—and even feel that the world belonged to us. And if parts of the Old World dreaded change, it was a stimulant to a young American; we could relish the latest pop songs and abstract art along with baroque music and ancient Egyptian sculpture; unlike some older Europeans, we saw no conflict there. Moreover, an American could be "the observant stranger" that James chose to become: "a complete outsider" likely to enjoy special insights. Training my eyes and ears, watching and listening, prepared me for the kinds of cultural history I was one day going to write.

In five years overseas my aesthete's self had been rewarded by seeing the black skies and golden fireworks of Whistler's Nocturnes at the Tate, the Sienese painters and Velázquez's long-limbed Venus at the National Gallery, Peggy Ashcroft as a lethal Hedda Gabler and John Gielgud (an entranced and outraged Benedick) in *Much Ado About Nothing,* Molière and Marivaux at the Comédie Française, sunsets in Venice and daybreak in Paris. I had seen the pigeons wheeling in circles above the Piazza San Marco, dipped my hands in the fountains of Aix-en-Provence, and wandered through the Roman Forum. I had been to Glyndebourne for *The Magic Flute,* had watched Benjamin Britten conducting his *Turn of the Screw,* and had sung six Bach motets in St. James's Church in Piccadilly. Marching into Trafalgar Square in the midst of a huge crowd opposing nuclear weapons, I had seen the sun strike the elegant spire of St. Martin-in-the-Fields, where I had heard Purcell's highest trumpets.

Henry Green believed that "we seldom learn directly; except in disaster, life is oblique in its impact on people." Perhaps. Yet I feel that I was given (unintended) guidance which was far from oblique. From Jane Howard I learned that betrayals are frequent and that masochism can be dangerous—and that life may be handsomely rebuilt upon the ruins. Koestler's autobiography had proved the existence of evil and how it had flourished in the twentieth century, and his personal history taught me about the determination to survive—until disease menaced him more fatally than the dictatorships of Franco, Hitler, and Stalin; the man who had often cheated death decided to summon it. A. J. Liebling showed me how reporting can be obsessive, almost as intoxicating as a love affair, especially among the byways of your own town, where the familiar becomes fascinating. John Davenport and Cyril Connolly exalted the splendors of the English language, the music and muscles of English prose. From Connolly I also learned to beware of predators who take protégés, and that bullying can backfire. Davenport's essays and Connolly's gave me literary touchstones, while the Frognal exiles made American history essential to me. (Schooled by the New Critics, I'd assumed that art and history or politics were mutually exclusive, that you couldn't be equally concerned with both, and I was grateful to discover that wasn't true.) Mai Zetterling proved what talent can achieve when it's harnessed to a soaring will, and that visual im-

ages can be as eloquent as words; early on, raised in a verbal universe, I hadn't known that. Tyrone Power showed that it was possible to change your life—even if the changes didn't last, they
could be wonderfully nourishing. And Kensington Court had
been a magical seedbed for a beginning writer, also a fine taking-
off place. Later I realized that it was strengthening too. Looking
back I see that I was drawn to dramatically different kinds of ex-
plorers—who had witnessed things I never had and never would.

And I wondered if they expressed aspects of myself: if I
harbored more than a trace of Jane's vulnerability, Koestler's
and Ella Winter's monumental selfishness, Liebling's outsize
ego, Davenport's and Connolly's snobbery and self-indulgence,
Power's elusiveness, Donald Ogden Stewart's naïveté as well as
his awareness of injustice. Unlike as all of them were, I could
identify with each one at moments—when it seemed as if they
spoke for me. Do those who intrigue or attract us also reflect
qualities that we're not proud of—but wouldn't choose to disown? And from others I learned that I wasn't good at decisions,
although life would demand making more and more of them.

From the blacklistees, I learned how the domestic Cold War
had ravaged my country—and for the first time I met people who
thought that the state of their nation was their business. Spending
time among them demystified the American Left for me; when
I heard others speak of radicals as destructive to democracy
or likely to inspire insurrections, I knew how foolish that was.
Most leftists had been horribly wrong about Russia, but in many
ways they had been right about the United States. While England
was telling me how much my homeland meant to me, I was also
learning more from the media about our homicidal racism and
the terrors it unleashed: the violent assaults on school desegrega-
tion, the children jeered at and spat on as they walked toward the
Little Rock Central High School, where crowds howled for their
blood, threatening to "lynch the niggers," and the beatings and
murders of black Americans, chiefly in the Deep South, where

trying to vote could mean losing your life. There had been "race riots" in the wretched slums of London's Notting Hill, where young white gangs attacked black immigrants with broken milk bottles, but that was hardly on a par with the savage resurgence of the Ku Klux Klan in the United States.

I also knew that my country was riddled with stifling conformities which inhibited many of the young. So my waxing sense of my American identity gave me no feelings of superiority. (The search for personal identity was paramount among young people of that period, and it was a recurrent theme in our literature.) In the years before Vietnam, we didn't yet see ourselves as international destroyers. Still, a good many Americans knew that we were exporting the crappiest parts of our mass culture—the TV game shows, clichés and mediocrities of all sorts—and prompting other countries to ape our commercialism. So while I grew more and more restless in England, I couldn't claim that life was better at home—just that I knew where my home was.

Long after London, surprises were in store for me. I hadn't known that some of the Frognal guests had once been Communists; in the late Fifties they could not say so without attracting further investigations. The journeys of most ex-Communists I met were similar: they'd joined the Party in the Thirties, resigned in the Forties, and were punished in the Fifties. Many went public in the Seventies about their former membership, especially after Watergate and Nixon's resignation. But some unaffiliated leftists took unpredictable turns. That Charlie Chaplin would one day pay his back taxes and revisit the United States—he wept during a standing ovation at Lincoln Center in 1972 and told the audience, "I'm being born again"—that Kingsley Amis and John Osborne would become right-wing reactionaries, all this would have seemed unimaginable in the Eisenhower/Harold MacMillan years. Part of my education was learning how wrong you can be—as well as how American I was.

And I learned how quickly convictions can appear to fade—

not among those who held them, but in the national ether. In the
Fifties the ideas of the radicals of the Thirties, who had aimed to
transform their own society, were known to few outside their
dwindling circle; I would have encountered them mainly in text-
books if I hadn't had tea at Frognal. Years later I followed the
trail of the American Left, intent on unearthing hidden history
that could get lost. And I thought how Koestler would have rejoiced at the 1989 revolutions in Eastern Europe and the collapse
of the Soviet Union. Yet might he have missed an enemy worthy
of his hate? He and the Frognal visitors would have been contemptuous of the Russian millionaires of the Nineties—cruising
Moscow in their Mercedes, dispensing bribes, abetting crooks.
But surely Koestler would have gloated over the humiliation of
the old Soviets by corrupt new capitalists. He and the American
leftists had fought oppression, although each would have defined
it very differently, while they regarded one another as monsters.
So much passion! Such fury! among those who were far from the
front lines. Yet many millions were miserably dead at a distance,
overseas: in the wake of ideologies that helped to kill them. I in-
tend no disrespect for the beliefs and the battles. But history in-
sists that nothing endures forever.

In our flat on Cheyne Walk I shored up reminders of New York:
a recording of *West Side Story,* guidebooks to the city, maps of
neighborhoods, big bright paper fish-kites from Manhattan's
Japanese stores. I wore my Bloomingdale's threads, sang "The
Bronx is up and the Battery's down" and "Officer Krupke" in the
bathtub, and after a binge of deep-garlic Provençal cooking, inspired by Elizabeth David's recipes, served meatloaf and Yankee
pot roast. And I was perversely pleased that the English appeared
to have little understanding of Thoreau and Whitman and

Melville: if parts of my literature were inaccessible to them, the independence of my heritage seemed all the more valuable.

I became difficult to live with, partly in hopes that my husband wouldn't wish to hold me in place. I didn't then realize that I was something of a brat, not spoiled—in many ways I was strictly brought up—but a mutinous young person, ready to rebel against almost anything. Repeatedly and most seriously he asked me to make a "sacrifice": to cut the cord that bound me to New York and to my country. I couldn't. Yet I felt horribly torn. So I plotted my escape with all the cunning of a prisoner, not perceiving that I wasn't really in jail. I was sure that we'd made a misalliance, I was also sure that we loved each other. He said I often murmured his name in my sleep, even after we'd been fighting. But I was positive that marriage—almost any marriage—would destroy love, and certain that I needed to live in my own town. Since I didn't believe that love could last, I began to want our marriage to end quickly. Wouldn't the pain be lessened if we parted soon? To him my feelings made no sense; he could not respect them and yet he wanted me to stay, tried hard to detain me. My fear of being imprisoned coexisted with a fear of abandonment. I thought I would soon be replaced by a more "rational" woman—whether I stayed or left. That wouldn't be Maria, but in a way Maria had won, as if she'd put a curse on us: he and I would not remain together.

Inevitably there was guilt and sadness—for having killed our closeness, for having uprooted love. Briefly I wondered if I'd followed the wrong path: the person who leaves almost always feels that way. But New York welcomed and rewarded me as I had expected. My roots slipped into the sidewalks, I was entirely at home: almost as though I'd never left. At times just walking along a Manhattan street could make me feel happy: striding quickly at high noon in blue-and-gold fall weather or strolling slowly within a large, loose crowd; even if I was low, a New York walk could raise my spirits.

Particular places—the crescent stone stairs of Carl Schurz Park by the East River, the hub of Grand Central beneath the signs of the zodiac on the ceiling, the plaza around the Bethesda Fountain—made me proud of the city that contained them. My relationship with the town was so personal that I shared its moods: angry during heatwaves and before Christmas, pensive at twilight, jubilant when our baseball team won the World Series and tons of ticker tape fell and flew. I felt possessive of my metropolis, even though I knew something about its cruelties and corruptions and knew that there was much worse to learn. But with a rush of powerful emotions, I was newly grateful to be there and to have grown up amid the fortresses and tenements, the turrets and brownstones. There were days when I felt I owned New York, and others when it seemed to own me—hence it wouldn't release me to live elsewhere.

Love and pain awaited me as well: there were men I liked very much and one I loved greatly. But the era would reshape my life even more than the men or the city. What lay ahead for me was an immersion in the Sixties and writing about the experiences of those years as they gained momentum. In the midst of a quarter of a million people, I heard Martin Luther King, Jr., describe the dream at the 1963 March on Washington, where he was sur- rounded by a sea of exultation. I began to feel that I was a partic- ipant in history and that my life was connected to others' who felt the same. The civil rights movement, the politics of protest, black militants and white radicals, and above all the Vietnam War, sent me into waves of tear gas in Chicago at the Democratic Conven- tion of 1968, into the massive crowds that ringed the Pentagon. I spent a long July Fourth weekend with the John Birch Society in Boston, where I do-si-doed at a square dance of the faithful, traveled to Fort Bragg in North Carolina, where I listened to GIs just returned from Vietnam, to Black Panther conferences in an Oakland, California park and a university gym in Philadelphia. With New York drug counselors I heard the mothers of heroin addicts comparing their sons' afflictions and sharing their own cynicism about treatment programs. I went to Watts, where singed alleys were still scarred from the firestorm of the ghetto's uprising, which left thirty-four people dead and some nine hundred injured, to campuses on strike against the war, where the smoke from burning draft cards mingled with the fumes of pot. In Washington I saw scores of Vietnam veterans in tattered uniforms and helmets unpinning their Purple Hearts and Bronze Stars and flinging them onto the steps of the Capitol; ribbons and stripes ripped from sleeves landed on the white marble, and the veterans shouted the names of their dead friends as they threw their own medals away. (They had brought their discharge papers so that no one could question their military service.) I witnessed the superbly organized forerunners of the Christian Coalition persuading people who had never voted to do so for the first time. And I watched the filming of confrontation scenes for a movie about "student revolution": the actors and extras kept arguing over the issues at hand while they waited to thrash each other before the cameras.

The counterculture took me to the lofts and church basements of Off-off-Broadway, where hallucinatory styles of performance —simultaneous screams and yells amid flashing strobe lights, dialogues in unison, naked bodies prancing down the aisles, scenes where everything is happening at once yet constantly changing—expressed the fragmentary nature of the period. In the summer of 1967, many young middle-class dropouts declared that they had no respect for money and didn't want straight jobs, while the "good vibrations" the Beach Boys sang about seemed more desirable than ever. (There were a few predictions that vibes would replace speech by the year 2000, when people would converse through all their senses rather than talking.) Between the hash pipes, acid was called "a binding substance" and some said it made them patient and tolerant; others spoke of paranoia. I visited the tribal communes of the East Village, where street dances and skits, free stew (and sometimes strawberry yogurt) served daily in Tompkins Square Park, far-flung psychedelia, poster-painting, and nimble clowning gave way to a plethora of drugs: lots of love beads got broken and rolled into cracks too deep to reach; horoscopes went awry and the moon betrayed Virgo.

In Miami Beach I saw President Richard Nixon glowing and beaming as he was nominated for a second term, and watched Allen Ginsberg arranging "a mystic marriage" ceremony between a group of elderly citizens and young ones, intoning, "The generation war is at an end." In Manhattan I listened to Ayn Rand hissing to a rapt audience that the United States had been damaged by altruism and "an orgy of self-sacrificing" (which would result in "slavery, brute force," and "sacrificial furnaces") and asserting that defending capitalism was "a *moral* issue," to Timothy Leary entreating his followers to "leave their minds behind" ("Turn on, tune in, drop out"), presidential candidate George Wallace hollering half-completed racist statements at an audience of sixteen thousand at Madison Square Garden. At a college for policemen I sat in on different classes where middle-aged cops discussed James Baldwin's *The Fire Next Time,* water imagery in Milton's *Lycidas*, and Freud ("too old-hat," they said). Asked to define a liberal, the classmates finally agreed on "obstructionist." At Kent State, five years after four students were accidentally shot dead by the National Guard, I heard remorse from professors and indifference from undergraduates, to whom the killings seemed as remote as the Peloponnesian War.

The conflicts of my country and my culture told me what to write: it seemed as though the themes chose me, rather than vice versa. But I never foresaw any of that as I packed my books and long-playing records and clothes on Cheyne Walk, bought my one-way air ticket, and was driven to the airport by a friend who was anxious about my future and about his. There would be rocks and fissures on the road ahead, but he shouldn't have worried about either of us.

The dolphin bore me gently to the shore, which gleamed as I approached it. As the recurring dream evaporated, I realized that I had fallen asleep in the plane which was carrying me home to New York. The floor throbbed beneath my feet as we began our descent: with the same eagerness that had taken me abroad, I leaned toward the small round window, craning my neck to see the towers of Manhattan.

# Acknowledgments and Sources

A grant from the Grand Street Foundation enabled me to revisit London to test my memories, and it freed my time to write this book: my great thanks to Ben Sonnenberg.

Parts of my first draft were written at Yaddo, the best possible working retreat, where privacy takes on a fresh significance: it means the privilege to concentrate on nothing but your calling.

Most of the details and quotes here come from the notebooks of my early twenties, and from my letters: I'm indebted to friends who were willing to return those inky airmails.

Once again I'm enormously grateful to Erik Wensberg for all sorts of editorial guidance. I thank Miles Huddleston and Ileene Smith for perusing early drafts, and James Harvey and David Hughes for reading certain chapters. Mervyn Jones provided invaluable historical background. So did Ellen Schrecker and Marvin Gettleman. Michele Slung gave me choice and welcome advice.

John T. Hill and Mary Clemmey arranged for certain photographs which would never have appeared here without their generous help.

For their recollections of the blacklist era I thank Arthur

Miller, Karen Morley, John Randolph, Wilma Shore Solomon, Gloria Stuart, Paul Sweezy, and Mary Yohalem.

My thanks to J. D. McClatchy and Susan Bianconi of *The Yale Review* and the Smart Family Foundation, and to Richard Poirier of *Raritan*.

And here are particular thanks to Molly Friedrich, my agent, and Paul Cirone.